ANTHONY
BURNS

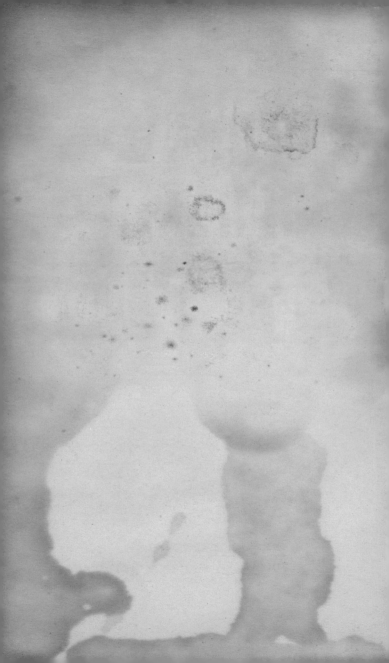

ANTHONY BURNS:

The defeat and triumph of a fugitive slave

by virginia hamilton

A KNOPF PAPERBACK

Alfred A. Knopf · New York

A KNOPF PAPERBACK PUBLISHED BY ALFRED A. KNOPF, INC.

Text copyright © 1988 by Virginia Hamilton
Cover art copyright © 1988 by Leo and Diane Dillon

All rights reserved under International and Pan-American Copyright Conventions.
Published in the United States of America by Alfred A. Knopf, Inc., New York, and
simultaneously in Canada by Random House of Canada Limited, Toronto.
Distributed by Random House, Inc., New York. Originally published in
hardcover as a Borzoi Book by Alfred A. Knopf, Inc., in 1988.

http://www.randomhouse.com/

Library of Congress Cataloging-in-Publication Data
Hamilton, Virginia.
Anthony Burns : the defeat and triumph of a fugitive slave / by Virginia Hamilton.
p.   cm.
Summary: A biography of the slave who escaped to Boston in 1854, was arrested at
the instigation of his owner, and whose trial caused a furor between abolitionists and
those determined to enforce the fugitive slave acts. Bibliography: p.   Includes index.
1. Burns, Anthony, 1834–1862—Juvenile literature. 2. Fugitive slaves—United States—
Biography—Juvenile literature. 3. Slavery—United States—Anti-slavery
movements—Juvenile literature. [1. Burns, Anthony, 1834–1862. 2. Fugitive slaves.
3. Slavery. 4. Afro-Americans—Biography.] I. Title.
E450.B93H36   1988   973.6'6'0924—dc19   [B]   [92]   87-38063

ISBN 0-394-98185-5 (lib. bdg.)
ISBN 0-679-83997-6 (pbk.)

First Knopf Paperback edition: January 1997
Printed in the United States of America
10 9 8 7 6

IN MEMORY OF
ANTHONY BURNS

THE ABOLITIONIST HYMN

We ask not that the slave should lie
As lies his master, at his ease,
Beneath a silken canopy,
Or in the shade of blooming trees.
We ask not "eye for eye," that all
Who forge the chain and ply the whip
Should feel their torture, while the slave
Should wield the scourge of mastership.
We mourn not that the man should toil,
'Tis nature's need, 'tis God's decree;
But let the hand that tills the soil
Be, like the wind that fans it, free.

—ANONYMOUS

Contents

List of Characters

R. A. BALL — Minister, St. Catharines, Canada

P. T. BARNUM — The showman, owner of Barnum's Hotel and Circus

JAMES BATCHELDER — The Marshal's guard killed during the storming of Boston Court House

WILLIAM BRENT — Southerner, Colonel Suttle's slave agent

HORACE W. BROWN — Witness, police officer, former carpenter

ANTHONY BURNS — Fugitive slave who ran away from Virginia to Boston, Massachusetts

ASA BUTMAN — Deputy U.S. Marshal known for capturing fugitive slaves

EBENEZER CALDWELL — Slave owner

BENJAMIN F. HALLETT	U.S. District Attorney
THOMAS WENTWORTH HIGGINSON	Minister and abolitionist from Worcester, Massachusetts
SAMUEL G. HOWE	Philanthropist and historian
SISTER JANETY	Slave owned by John Suttle, sister of Anthony Burns
WILLIAM JONES	Witness, employer of Anthony Burns at Mattapan Works, South Boston
EDWARD GREELEY LORING	Judge of Probate, Commissioner for taking bail and affidavits, presiding over slave cases
ROBERT LUMPKIN	Slave trader, owner of Lumpkin's Jail
LUTHER	Slave owned by Charles Suttle
MAMAW	Slave owned by John Suttle, mother of Anthony Burns
MAUDE MAW	Slave, a "two-head": a seer said to know the future
MR. AND MRS. DAVID McDANIEL	Slave owners
MR. MILLSPAUGH	Druggist, hired Anthony Burns in Richmond, Virginia
ROBERT MORRISS	Abolitionist lawyer

EDWARD G. PARKER	Lawyer for Charles Suttle
THEODORE PARKER	Abolitionist, minister of 28th Congregational Society, Tremont Temple
WENDELL PHILLIPS	Abolitionist lawyer, orator, and crusader for human rights
FRANKLIN PIERCE	14th President of the United States, 1853–57
COFFIN PITTS	Deacon, 12th Baptist Church of Boston, friend and employer of Anthony Burns
DEPUTY MARSHAL JOHN H. RILEY	One of the Marshal's men guarding Anthony Burns
MR. RUSSELL	Employer of William Jones
GEORGE R. RUSSELL	Presiding at Faneuil Hall public meeting, Friday, May 26, 1854
SHADRACH	Fugitive slave, captured but escaped from Boston Court House, 1851
SIMON	Slave owned by Charles Suttle
THOMAS SIMS	Fugitive slave, captured by As· Butman in 1851, tried and re turned to slavery
J.V.C. SMITH	Mayor of Boston
G. S. STOCKWELL	Northern minister who discov-

	ered whereabouts of Anthony Burns, 1855
MARTIN STOWELL	Abolitionist from Worcester, Massachusetts
CHARLES F. SUTTLE	Son of John Suttle, Colonel in Virginia Militia, owner of Anthony Burns
JOHN SUTTLE	Called he Mars, father of Charles Suttle, owner of child Anthony Burns, Mamaw, Big Walker, Janety, etc.
MISTRESS SUTTLE	Called she Missy, wife of John Suttle, owner of slaves
JOHN SWIFT	Young lawyer
CHIEF OF POLICE TAYLOR	Boston, 1854
SETH J. THOMAS	Lawyer for Charles Suttle
BEN TRUE	Witness, guard over Anthony Burns
BIG WALKER	Possibly Anthony Burns's father; driver, or foreman, of John Suttle's slaves
JAMES T. WHITTEMORE	Witness; member, Boston City Council, and a lieutenant in the Pulaski Guards
WHITTOM	Slave owned by Charles Suttle

ANTHONY BURNS

1

MAY 24, 1854

"HOLD ON, boy!" A harsh voice called to him from the dim light on Brattle Street.

He held himself in and managed to sound calm when he asked, "What do you want of me?"

"They say a boy broke into the jewelry store," the man said, and walked nearer. "About twenty hours ago it was that a boy took a valuable piece of silver. And you look like the same boy."

"I never stole in my life!" he exclaimed. He knew he couldn't have been the one. He was no boy. But something inside him cautioned, *Steal away to Jesus!* "I haven't ever stole," he said evenly.

"Let's just see about it, m'boy," the man said. "Let's just walk down to the Court House."

He panicked and started to run. Men came out of the shadows to surround him. He bolted, but they caught him and lifted him off his feet. They carried him like a corpse at the height of their shoulders. He did next what he knew how to do: He closed his eyes and went far inside himself. Gripped tightly by these strangers up on their shoulders, he stayed stiffly in their hands.

There seemed to be a leader and maybe six others. He thought, They are like pallbearers—am I a dead man? They've caught me, but I'm not a thief. They say I *stole*. I know I have stole nothing in my life!

He was innocent. That was why he had resisted and run. He'd been on the corner of Brattle and Court Streets, coming from his work at Mr. Pitts' clothing store. In view was Faneuil Hall, the old market building. It had been built with money earned from selling West Indian slaves. Now it was used by Christian abolitionists who in the present year, 1854, prayed and preached against slavery. So he had been told by his employer and friend, the freeman Coffin Pitts.

The men who had caught him continued to carry him on their shoulders to Boston Court Square and the Court House.

They've mixed me up with some poor soul, he was thinking. It's all a mistake. Keep yourself quiet, make no resistance, he told himself. He didn't move a muscle.

Breathing heavily, perspiring, the men took a moment's rest when they arrived at the Court House. Once inside, they stood him on his feet. He opened his eyes and looked at them hard just for a moment. They looked rough to him, like the lowest types; so did the leader.

They lifted him up again and carried him to a jury room on the third floor. There, with some relief, they set him down again.

He brushed and straightened his clothing to proper or-

4

der and looked around for the jewelry store owner; instead, he saw the door closing, shutting him in. There were iron bars set in the door. The windows, too, had iron bars over them. And the men who had carried him now stood silently to either side of the barred door.

Suddenly he felt like a caged animal. Fear chilled his neck. What was this all about? But he kept his expression aloof. He'd show them he wasn't afraid.

Never let a buckra—never let a man who is white—know what you are thinking.

This was the axiom that he and all of his kind had learned to live by.

The barred door of the room swung open suddenly. The men came smartly to attention, their hands resting lightly on the guns in their belts.

Men with guns. How came so many buckras upon him? Now entered three more. One was a stranger to him. But the other two he recognized at once. The sight of them shocked him, stunned him, and made his heart thud violently.

"Go in, go in," he told himself. "Go inside where they will not follow. Go! The Lord and his light alone can reach you."

Charles F. Suttle of Virginia entered the jury room with his agent, William Brent. He came over to the prisoner, Anthony Burns. Mockingly, Colonel Suttle bowed low to him. "How do you do, *Mistah* Burns!" he said. "Why did you run away from me! Haven't I always treated you well?" His north-country-Virginia accent was as thick and sweet as molasses.

5

Anthony Burns heard the Colonel's words from a great distance. His spirit drew away, as water will seep into the ground and disappear. Buried memories rose from Anthony Burns's depths as he heard Mars Charles Suttle's voice. Mars Charles Suttle was the only son of he Mars John Suttle, who had owned Anthony as a boy. Mars Charles Suttle had inherited Anthony from Missy Suttle.

"I . . . I . . . fell asleep on board of the vessel where I worked," Anthony murmured finally, "and before I woke up she set sail and carried me off."

Colonel Suttle and Brent watched Anthony closely. They saw his eyes cloud and grow dim and his mouth draw down in despair. He was going within himself, to a place where no one could reach him, least of all Mars Charles.

Seeing this, Charles Suttle snickered, "Don't run away from me, Tony. He will do that, you know, Marshal Freeman," he told the man with the sword, "just like he's addle-brained." He turned again to Anthony. "Tony, haven't I always given you money when you needed it?"

Mars Suttle's distant voice made Anthony feel like a helpless child. And like a child, he responded, "You have always given me . . . twelve and a half cents . . . at Christmas—once a year!"

Mars Suttle smiled, and Anthony knew he had admitted too much. But what did it matter now? He was all alone. And he went far away within, as far back as the first memories he had of knowing what it meant to be Anthony Burns and somebody else's property.

"Well, now, that's the one, is it?" asked Marshal Freeman—a thin man whose face was pitted with smallpox scars. He was the United States Marshal, and the armed guards around Anthony had been hired by him.

"Yes, suh, it's my property, certainly," Colonel Suttle answered proudly. Then, without another glance at Anthony, he walked out of the jury room, followed by the Marshal and Brent.

Anthony was not aware Suttle had gone anywhere, for he had left first and gone deep inside himself, to his childhood. There days seemed endless, perfect. There mornings and waking up were the times he could hardly wait for, he loved them so. . . .

SPRING 1839

HE AWAKENED with his raggedy self curled upon the dirt floor. Around him were his sister's children, deep asleep. He was smaller than the others at the age of five, but he had the children in his charge from dusk to dawn. His sister had told him so.

"Anthony," she had said, "you will get them up and you will put them to bed."

"I makin' 'em resters," he told his sister. But the children didn't want his pillow resters. On lying down they shunned all contact with him. They despised him because he never had to work hard. Every sundown they came home exhausted. They cradled their heads on thin arms and fell asleep at once, too tired to want anything. More often than not they cried fretfully in their sleep throughout the night.

"Shhh. Shhhh," Anthony would soothe them.

And he would wake the children very early so they could go to labor. They never wanted to go, and they talked back to him about it. He didn't have to go, himself. He took care of his sister's baby, and he was happy

8

doing that. He didn't mind a babe at all. Often he would carry her upon his shoulder as he loped about the place. Or rock her cradle with his bare toes.

His mamaw was no longer close by. She had her own cabin farther along, where she bred her own babies just as his sister did. He wasn't allowed to go there often, and he did not dwell on the fact that he was left without Mamaw. He had about ten or eleven other brothers and sisters scattered all over the place. They were older, as was his sister. He lived away with the younger children, his cousins, alone in a cabin.

Anthony looked quickly around the cabin now. He saw the children, like heaps of rags. Their spindly legs, ashy and caked with dirt, were drawn up close. He had his own pillow that he hugged under him, and it was the best one he'd ever made. He'd used bunches of sweet grasses and bark, and something of his that was secret. All of it wrapped in a rag and tied with twine. An old mamaw he'd followed home one day had showed him how to start his pillow rester.

Now he lifted his head higher and looked out the door. Misty out, still not quite dayclean, the best time. He called the white dew on the ground summer snow.

No Big Walker, he thought. No overdoer come get the chil'ren yet.

All the children older than he had to be up at dawn. Anthony didn't have to, but he liked to be, else he would miss the most important time of his day. Each predawn that woke him with its first light made him feel he had awakened to life.

And here was the day, riding swiftly yellow, brightly

racing over the fields. It made him giggle to see it coming. He whispered loudly to the children on the cabin floor. "Wake up! Jim and Janety!" He was copying he Mars's way of naming them. These were not their real names. If they were boys, he Mars John Suttle, the boss man, called them Jim. If they were girls, he Mars called them Janety. The children knew which one he was calling by the one he Mars looked hard at. They watched his darting eyes, and they would know when to step up or jump aside. Anthony alone was spared this. He had been named by he Mars himself.

Behind the sunlight came the overdoer, Big Walker, called Driver by those who hated him most.

"Up, Jim and Janety!" Anthony called louder to the children. "Big Walker comin' after y'all."

They didn't argue. Still half asleep, they scrambled to their feet.

Big Walker was there among the cabins, crashing his fist against the doors and walls. He yelled loudly, and there was no playing with that voice: "Up and up and up! I say it's u-u-up time! You get up now. Bein' time to move! U-u-up ti-iiime!" He was the one who watched them and did good for them and bad to them if need be in the fields.

They got up, slipping out, hurrying every which way, trying not to get in the way of grown folks as they went. Cornbread was thrust into their hands. "Here's your Johnny Constant," old Jim, the food handler, would say, putting the cornbread into their hands as they hurried by.

The children kept their heads bowed, which was the way. They would eat the Johnny Constant along the paths to the fields. Maybe they'd get something more in a few hours. Perhaps some Billy Seldom, which was what they called the buttermilk biscuits that they loved, and something to drink. But now they had to go and eat Johnny as fast as they could.

All went, except for Anthony. His older sister came, holding her babe. She was dressed in Mistress's silken dressing gown that had been given over for her serving meals. "Bow down, Anthony," she murmured to him. "He comin'."

She bowed her head and held the baby close. Anthony became excited when he heard horse's hooves. "First come the mornin'," eagerly he told her, "then come Big Walker. Now come he Mars!"

"Hush, Anthony!" Sister Janety had no time to tell him again to bow down. Mars John Suttle's pony was upon them.

"Mornin' suh," his sister said respectfully to the boss man on the horse. It was the owner of the fields himself.

"Mo'nin, Janety," he Mars said in his thick voice. "How you by this mo'nin?"

"Good mornin' all oveh," she murmured. She had spoken softly to her chest, for her head was way bowed down. He Mars liked that. And she fell to her knees right there on the hard ground with the babe held tightly to her.

Anthony jumped up and down, beside himself with happiness. He saw he Mars look sharply beyond him. And before he could turn, he was lifted in hands like shovels. Anthony knew the hands, the muscled, huge arms. Big Walker held him up and turned him around. Anthony was still smiling when Big Walker slapped him

11

across his mouth. "Wipe that grin off—I say wipe it. And bow you head the way you s'pose to," he told Anthony. Then Walker turned back around toward he Mars.

"You got too much spirit, I believe, boy," he Mars Suttle told Anthony. "You see me a-comin', you bow you down like Janety there. Now bow down!"

Holding Anthony between his hands, Big Walker bowed himself and Anthony, too, from the waist. Anthony's feet were up off the ground, but still he bowed. He stayed bowed until Big Walker unbowed him. Until he Mars said it was all right for Big Walker to stand up and lift Anthony to the pony's neck.

That was where Anthony wanted to go. He would've gone, too, right away if only he hadn't forgot the rule and been slapped for it by the driver.

He Mars took Anthony out of Walker's arms and placed him comfortably on the front of the saddle.

As he was lifted, Anthony remembered not to look directly into he Mars John Suttle's face. For he Mars considered that worse than forgetting to bow. Anthony knew what he Mars looked like, anyhow. An elder man, so Mamaw said. He Mars's hair was almost gone from his head. And what was there was all white. The hair above his lip was white, too, and yellowish, and usually full of shortnin' johnnycake crumbs. Anthony knew what the crumbs were because Mamaw labored in the Suttle kitchen. She always put her shortnin' johnny to rise on a long board leaned by the fire hearth. She made the johnnycakes. Anytime Anthony wanted a piece, he ran up there and got it.

Everybody said Anthony was "spoilt." Even Missy

Suttle said so, crossly. He guessed "spoilt" was good, for everybody smiled when they said that he was, except for Missy. Sometimes, in a secret between him and Mamaw, he took a whole cake back to the cabin and the children. They weren't so jealous then that he was spoilt. They patiently waited for him to scoop up a handful for each of them.

He Mars slapped him lightly on his bare knees below the simple cotton sacking he wore. It was not lost on Anthony which one treated him more harshly—Big Walker or he Mars. And to himself he thanked he Mars for being there, else Big Walker might've hurt him more.

"There, you see?" Mars Suttle said to Walker. "The best management of my property is the keepin' of good discipline."

"Yay suh," Big Walker murmured.

"I say what?" he Mars asked.

"Good man'gement, good dis'pline," Big Walker said.

"There you have it," he Mars said. "You hear that, boy?" he said to Anthony.

Anthony nodded. Swiftly, Big Walker reached up and slapped him a stinging blow. It brought tears to his eyes, and a burning hatred for the big black man. Anthony whimpered once, but that was all. He wouldn't cry out.

"Now, now, Anthony," he Mars soothed him. "Walker didn't mean nothin'. But he hates to have anyone, even a favorite chile like you, forget his proper respect. Say what you have been taught to say when I speak to you."

"Yay suh, no suh," Anthony managed in a tiny voice, gulping tears.

"Uh-uh, now I told you that 'yay' and 'suh' nonsense is

13

fo' my field property. My house property says like this: 'Yay-es *sur*.' You see, the field cain't do it. Big Walker cain't. But you can, Anthony. Say it now, properly: 'Yay-es sur.' "

"Yays-surah," Anthony said, the best an almost-six-year-old piece of property could do.

The man sighed. "That will do fine. Just remember, boy, that under Gawd I am your lawgiver and your judge."

"Yays-surah!"

Then, coolly, he Mars studied Big Walker. "Love and fear," he murmured. "Reason, gratitude, obedience, shame." He grinned at Big Walker. "Now ain't you ashamed to be hittin' a po' little one like-a that!"

"Yay suh!" Big Walker said instantly, eyes downcast.

"So you see, Anthony," said he Mars, "Walker feelin' ashamed of himself for hittin' you. He don't mean to. But you must never again give him cause. You must think, and be thankful that you are taken care of. Do right the first time. Remember that, Anthony."

Anthony remembered. "Yays-surah," he said softly.

"Then, let's ride!" he Mars said. And they rode. Gone were Anthony's tears and hurt. Oh, how he loved a strutting pony! Sitting there in the most favored place in front of he Mars himself, as long as Mars' own boy, Charles, was off in school, made Anthony instantly, completely, happy.

They rode in the early morning. For he Mars did not care to have neighbors see him ride holding Anthony on the saddle with him. It was all right if his own property saw, but that was all. He Mars never paid much attention to Anthony at other times. But when they rode, it was as

14

if the two of them were in a world of their own. He Mars than held Anthony close and would brush Anthony's cheek with his own while talking to him.

The field and house word was that Anthony was he Mars Suttle's own boy. It was a fact that Mamaw labored in the Suttle kitchen, cooking all the food for the big house and the field hands and taking care of he Mars's sitting room and Master's bedroom. Missy Suttle had her own upstairs maid.

It was true, Anthony's skin was lighter than that of most property. And his mamaw was indeed a breeder woman. She was made to have a baby each year so that he Mars would increase his holdings. Still, nobody knew for certain whether Anthony was he Mars John Suttle's second son. Word along the cabin row was that the big, tall Walker was who he belonged to.

But Anthony knew nothing of this.

They rode. Anthony was in paradise. He could smell the pony. He could smell the scent that he Mars poured onto his pocket cloth each morning. A clean handkerchief it was that Anthony's mamaw had readied for him, all ironed and starched, just the same as she prepared his riding clothes. Nobody touched he Mars's clothes but Mamaw. And it was she who put the scented cloth in his pocket.

It wasn't an enormously large estate that Mars and Mistress Suttle owned. But it was big enough to keep Anthony and Mamaw and all her thirteen children. It kept his sister's and hers.

"If we havin' be someplace," Mamaw said, "this ole place ain' worser than any."

Soon paradise came to its end. When he Mars questioned him about what he had seen, Anthony knew the time to ride was almost over.

"I seen all I wanted," Anthony told him. "Yays-surah, I seen the chickens. I seen the cows and the horses. I seen fields and barns. Woods, too."

"And what about the rest of my property, Anthony? What about them in the fields, watering the horses and plowing; those feeding the chickens and milking the cows. And your own Mama Janety householding for Mistress?"

Anthony took his time to think. He was smart, and so he remembered. "I seen all them," he said carefully. He knew he Mars to be full of tricks. Anthony stayed alert and ready.

"You seen my own other property, Anthony?"

"Yays-surah!"

"Like cows and horses, what do you say, Anthony?"

"Yays-surah!"

"And what are they called, Tony, boy? What are they all called?"

"Slaves!" he said triumphantly. He'd got beyond all he Mars's tricks. And he was safe. "Slaves. They callum slaves."

"Right you are, lad," Suttle murmured, nuzzling Anthony's neck. But then, more sternly, he said, "*My* slaves, boy."

"Yays-surah, they yo' slaves. They my slaves, too," Anthony told him.

"Wh-what?" Mars Suttle peered down in shock at Anthony.

"Yays-surah! They Mamaw and sisterahs Janety and

16

brotherahs Jims—all them chil'ren," Anthony said. "They yo' slaves and they mine, too."

Suttle was so taken by surprise that he threw back his head and roared with laughter. "Gawd Almighty! You mean . . ." he sputtered, ". . . you are the same . . . You think . . . they are slaves . . . but you . . ." He bellowed, shaking all over. "Well, that is one of the completest mistakes you've evah made, Tony, m'boy, Gawd in heaven, it is!"

Anthony was confused as to what he Mars meant. But since he knew the words "Gawd" and "Heaven," he gathered it was at least partly Bible business.

"I will let it go for now, boy," he Mars said. He laughed again to himself. "Perhaps we'll just use this terrible mistake for a prayer lesson."

Because Virginia law forbade them to learn to read the Good Book, or any other book for that matter, John Suttle made it a strict rule never to have reading in the house in the presence of property. But he was forward-looking enough to allow churchgoing for his slaves; they attended the same Baptist church he did. There was a partition, of course, but property was given the opportunity to sing and to pray. Oh, they did love that!

"Lordy, wait till folks hear this one. Tony, m'boy, I knew you were keen witted but never so much as this! Haw-haw! You'll learn! Or die tryin'! I've hope for you, and profit, too. There's no limit to what you can be taught."

He gave Anthony a pat on his head, pulled his downy curls a moment, and checked to see if there were lice near the scalp. "I see Janety keepin' you clean, hum?"

"Yays-surah," Anthony said, sleepily enjoying the attention. He leaned comfortably back against he Mars.

"Like you mama before you," he Mars mused. "Respect and gratitude and strength of mind. Yes, my property! Mine!" He laughed, and without warning flung Anthony down from the pony to the ground. Anthony managed to cushion the fall somewhat by doing a somersault.

"Good lad!" he Mars said.

Anthony remembered to right himself and show no shock or pain at being tossed so brutally. He Mars waited. Anthony remembered what was important. Again he bowed deeply.

"And now you know, don't you, boy?" he Mars said. "Anthony, you my property, you belong to *me*. You my own slave chile." Said with tight emotion. With that, he Mars turned the pony and rode away, more important things at once on his mind.

Anthony stared after him, half in longing and half in fear and wonder. The meaning of he Mars's last words would come to him slowly, over time.

3

MAY 24, 1854

THE INNOCENT child of five slipped away. Anthony stirred. Layer by layer, he returned to his miserable time of manhood in the year 1854. He found himself with the ones who had seized him this night on Brattle Street. They had cuffed his hands with irons connected by chains. How had they done that?

But I was daydreaming, Anthony thought. He lifted his hands to look at the chains. They felt so heavy, he let them drop. "Wish all this was a dream, like that vision of when I was small," he told himself. It was more like a nightmare. Chains!

The leader of the men introduced himself. "Call me Asa Butman," he said. "I am Deputy United States Marshal and known for catching runaway property!"

The guards, growing rowdy, guffawed, and Asa smiled. "I caught a slave named Thomas Sims back in fifty-one," Asa said, "and I held him in this very same room as I holdin' you, Burns."

Anthony mumbled, "You said you arrested me for stealing."

Asa chuckled, then stopped when he saw Burns's shockingly maimed right hand. The skin over the protruding bone was drawn tight and shone like satin. Asa assumed, as did everyone who saw the hand, that the slaveholder, Charles Suttle, had abused him horribly.

Anthony saw Asa's eyes on his hand but didn't try to explain what had happened. For a fleeting moment he recalled the accident that had injured his hand when he was about thirteen. The awful memory paled next to the shuddering fear he faced now, and his thoughts raced over the events leading to his capture.

After work that day he'd been following Coffin Pitts over to the church pastored by Reverend Leonard Grimes, where Mr. Pitts was deacon. The church was new, and was known locally as the church of the fugitive slaves in Boston. Anthony had refused to go at first because he felt he had no right. He wrote to his church in Virginia seeking a formal release from its communion so that he would be free to join Reverend Grimes's church. But his Virginia pastor refused, saying that Anthony had disobeyed God's law by running away from his master. He was "excommunicated," the pastor had written, "from the community and fellowship of the church." Therefore, Anthony could join no other church, ever.

Back home Mars Charles had let him preach. Now he would be as nothing in the eyes of God.

I should have gone on with Deacon Pitts in the first place, Anthony thought. We had left the shop for the day.

I had started home. And if I hadn't had a change of heart and followed after him, there would have been the two of us. Maybe then the guards would have feared to take me.

I oughtn't to have written my church.

For he had written to his brother there in Virginia; the authorities must have got it out of his brother where he had gone.

Yes, and I am here in jail as proof.

Over the course of the evening, Asa Butman and his guards were friendly enough. Anthony appeared listless, although he listened to Butman's every word.

"Ever you hear tell of the Fugitive Slave Act?" Asa Butman asked him, leaning close. The guards listened.

Anthony raised himself slightly, blinking as though his brain was muddled. He knew how to pretend to be dull minded whenever it was to his advantage to hide himself and his feelings from the buckras.

"Now try to stay awake, Anthony," Butman said. "Ya see, it's like this, m'boy. It is 'Anniversary Week' here in Boston city. The ab-o-litionists—thems against slavery—and the woman suf-fra-gists—after the vote for womens—and the rest of them kind is having their yearly conventions.

"Every boarding place is crowded up," Asa went on. "When what happens? Two upstanding gen'mens from Virginia, Colonel Charles F. Suttle and his slave agent, Billy Brent, ride right into town and set themselves up in style at the Revere House hotel. Now it's dangerous for them here with Boston full of their enemies. But by Gawd, m'boy, not one ab-o-litionist was looking the right way!"

The guards snickered, then laughed outright. "And we took you, m'boy, right off the street, right under Deacon Pitts's nose! And we had a right," Asa said. "That Fugitive Act means a runaway can get captured in any free state—even Massachusetts."

"Hear, hear!" said the guards. They gave Butman light applause, for it was obvious he was showing off for Anthony.

"All the slave owner needs," Butman continued, "is to supply a affi-davit saying who is the one wanted. In your case, you!"

"Then the U.S. Commissioner, Judge Edward Loring, the speaker there at Harvard Law School," Asa said, "he issues a fugitive slave warrant. It was given me by the Marshal, and I is the one arrests you."

The guards applauded wildly. "And we helped him, we did," one of them joined in. They were the *posse comitatus*, so named in the slave act as aiding the commissioner and the marshal in the execution of their duties. The marshal had assembled them and paid them well to help him keep the peace. All were lowlifes and petty thieves, the only kind of men who in 1854 would take on the task of capturing runaway slaves.

"Well, I reckon that Fugitive Slave Act fixes it for *all* you runnin'-away kind," continued Asa. " 'Cause now the Commissioner can issue a certificate to send you on back where you come from." He grinned. "The Commissioner gets ten dollars if he convicts you, but only a fiver if he acquits."

Anthony listened. He felt sick inside. Asa's words broke his heart.

They will take me back! Anthony thought. There's law against me. Lord, I'm lost.

"There you have it, m'buy," Asa said to him.

Anthony shrank in his shell, speaking to no one.

"Come on, m'boy," Asa told him. "Have a drink and some food on me. Oh, don't take on so! It ain't half bad. You'll go back and take your whippin' and ole Colonel will forget all about it!"

But Anthony knew that if he went back, things would not go well for him at all. He dared not dwell on what would happen.

Where is Deacon Pitts? Does he not question where I be? Anthony wondered. And good Reverend Grimes? Oh, no. I did tell the deacon I wasn't coming to church. He never knew I followed him. Never saw me taken there in the dark. No one knows I'm caught!

Anthony cringed. He let his mind drift away on the floating pain inside him. And discovered the boy Anthony again, the innocent child.

4

SUMMER 1841

"HOW OLD are you now?" Anthony asked the boy.

"Almost seven."

"Ah, yes," Anthony said. "John Suttle dies all a-sudden about this time. That was the last pony ride you'll ever have."

"I love pony rides," said the boy. "When I'm good, he Mars let me hold the reins."

"Missy Suttle will have charge of Mars John's slaves now," Anthony told him. "She's not so kind. Beatings and threats! She'll sell some of your brothers and sisters to pay off debts."

The child of seven sat by a stream, fishing. He had a swaddled new baby among the leaves next to him. It was his sister's newborn infant. What Anthony said frightened him.

Then, soon after, came another time of childhood. It was night, after the children had stumbled home in the dark from their labor. Anthony had given them water, sourdough bread with a little bacon and grease, and black molasses to sop the bread in. He'd taken the food from

Mamaw's kitchen in the good house—his own name for he Mars and she Missy's place. He remembered what Mamaw had told him when he'd asked for sweets and cake.

"Things change," she had said. Tears were in her eyes.

"Somebody sick?" he'd asked.

"Yay-ah, somebody. Was," Mamaw answered. And he knew. It came to him suddenly that he had not seen he Mars John Suttle for some time. That was both good and bad. It meant that Big Walker wouldn't be around so much. But it was bad that he never rode he Mars's pony now.

"He Mars gone away?"

"Mars gone an' set beside King Jesus. You 'member Jesus, Anthony, in church."

"*A little talk wid Jesus make it right.*" Softly, he sang part of a hymn Mamaw had taught him.

His mamaw took up another melody. "*Way down yonder in the graveyard walk, I thank Gawd ah'm free at last!*" All at once she grabbed up the hems of her long skirts and commenced to sidestep and sway. "*Me and m'Jesus gwoin' meet an' talk, I thank Gawd ah'm free at last!*" She pranced forward and back.

Young Anthony laughed, joining in. Dancing in praise of the Lord was the way of the cabin row. "You lookin' like a gobbler with she feathers held low!" he told Mamaw.

She smiled. Three times she had jumped the broom, a custom in marriage, and had thirteen children. Life was hard, but it was still life. "*Some o' these mornins, bright an' fair*—come on, Anthony!"

"Comin'." He stepped and pranced. Thumbs hooked to his sides, he kept his elbows back and his chest out. It wasn't easy keeping time with Mamaw. *"I thank Gawd ah'm free at last!"* he sang.

"Gwoin' meet Jesus in the middle of the air, I thank Gawd ah'm free at last!" Mamaw finished, and sat down.

In a moment she caught her breath. "Oh, Anthony!" She drew him to her. "I pray that one day you be in the church. You preach for all us, from the Bible."

"Yay, Mamaw, I do it. Soon's I larn readin'."

"I pray that," she said, and held him close. She whispered, "You still a-huntin' and gatherin' the scraps?"

"What I can find," he said. "I pick up and keep 'em."

"Don't let Sister's chil'ren or anyone know, Anthony. Not even when it's all gathered and done."

"I won't, Mamaw. I keep all it by me close."

"You a good chile," Her voice trembled. She held him so tight, it hurt him. He knew she feared for him, but he didn't know why. Was it because Mars John was gone now?

That was how he and Mamaw had been just a short time ago in the kitchen of the good house. Now young Anthony lay in the dark in the cabin with his head on his pillow rester. He squeezed it between his hands, listening to it rustle. Among the leaves and grasses of its filling were hidden the scraps of paper he had found with writing and printing on them. He had a whole collection of scraps now. Some had marks that were just alike. He knew a number of the markings. And someday he'd know what they said. Once he could read the markings, he figured he could read the Bible. For the Bible had the same kind of markings. Then Mamaw would be very pleased with him.

All reading was secret—he didn't know why yet. Mamaw gave him thrown-away pieces of letters and printing from the good house. And all such scraps he saved inside his pillow, to look over when he could snatch a moment alone. His pillow grew softer, fuller over time.

"Never let the buckras know what you got there," Mamaw had told him.

"Not he Mars?"

"No."

"Not she Missy?"

"Lord, no!"

Now it was deep in the dark night. He'd fed the children and they slept again. He must've dozed. Suddenly he was wide awake, lifting his head to listen. He stayed half alert even when he was dreaming. What he'd first heard he now heard again. A slight sound, a creaking, like a cabin door closing.

Don't let Walker hear it! he thought.

There was silence again. He waited for what seemed forever. Looked all around him. No other child stirred. Carefully, Anthony reached out and opened the door just enough so he could peek.

Dark night. It made him shiver, but it was exciting, too.

"Go out," he told himself.

Then he heard it. Not far. A cabin down the row, closer to the woods.

He got up and carefully opened the door so it was just big enough for him to slip through. Night slid in around him and poured its inky black over him. It covered him, made him unseen. He was out with the dark. There was no breeze. He followed the shapes of cabins against the night. He was so small, with eager eyes hidden by dark.

All the houses of the row were the same crude dwellings. Dirt floors. Chinks of windows between the logs and mud daubings, with burlap and tree bark over the chinks. Some entrances had only holey blankets for doors. He could make out the men's cabin and the old men's cabin. Next was the women's cabin and the breeder women's cabin—in the same row but separated by a stand of trees. Breeder women's cabin was where Mamaw and Sister Janety lived with babies under five years old.

Slight sounds almost hidden in the noise of insects led him beyond the row.

All at once he stopped dead in the dark. Waiting, listening. Somebody was coming. A mighty strength rushed by him, never seeing Anthony so small, hugging a cabin front for safety.

Trembling, Anthony made himself move on to the place where the row ended. Here began the forest surrounding all of he Mars John Suttle's place. Here was the forbidden land of terrifying sounds and pungent smells of piney wood. Pine-tar fumes made Anthony's eyes tear. This was where the wind lived. It stole forth, Mamaw said, making the cabins shrink close in icy winter daylight.

In the deep, dark forest dwelled wild animals and giant creatures that fed upon slaves who would run. So he and all the children were warned by she Missy. And they believed it.

Never run away. Hear tell of running, tell she Missy. Never enter the forest, else you will get eaten up. Wolves will sink teeth in your insides, and shake and swallow them. Your guts will steam out on the cold ground.

Tell, tell Missy.

In front of Anthony, up against the forest on slightly higher ground, was Big Walker's cabin. It was away from the row, as if Walker's back was against the forest. As if he was to guard the winding path from one place to another, guard against the cabin folk.

Anthony couldn't believe he had come so far all by himself in the dark. It had to be Big Walker's creaking door he'd heard opening and closing. Big Walker, rushing by Anthony on his way to home, late from hard labor in he Mars's stone quarry.

Somebody walkin' right in Walker's place, Anthony thought. A lot of somebodys.

He saw light, movement. There. Door opening, creaking its sound, and closing again. Anthony moved, more afraid standing still than moving. Just see the light in Walker's place, he thought. Go on up there. Stay low. Chinks there to see.

He saw through a chink. He eyes grew big. So many folks there, sitting close. Some swayed in the light of a tallow candle. They hummed such a soft sound. Comfort in humming together.

"And din't it rain?" Mumbly sounds in a rush of whispers. He knew that sound of sorrow meant trouble was near.

Candlelight flickered. Pale yellow, tallow light. Nobody had such light except in she Missy's good house. Mamaw must've got it. Walker couldn't get such tallow by himself. There—Mamaw!

29

Mamaw, in Walker's house?

Big Walker, moving around. Touching everybody—a shoulder here, bowed head there. Walker, bending over them like he cared about everybody.

Anthony looked on in awe. Big Walker! Actin' like he some all right. He some the same as we be.

Walker made his way over to the fire. He crouched low beside Mamaw. She laid her head on his shoulder, and Anthony went cold inside. Big Walker held Mamaw's hand and put his arm around her. They rocked together, back and forth.

Mamaw? Big Walker? Folks going to them and holding both them.

"Mamaaaw!" Anthony cried in agony at what he was seeing. Before he knew what was happening, the cabin door creaked and somebody got him. Lifted him and carried him inside. "It's Anthony." He was put down.

"Anthony!" Mamaw called. She held out her arms to him. He rushed to her. "Oh, Anthony."

"Better that he do hear. That he know everything now," Big Walker said.

Anthony began to cry, he was so confused. He could feel the sadness all around the room. "Hush, hush, now," Mamaw told him.

Mamaw began talking. She held his head against her, had his ears in her palms. He buried his face in her neck.

"Say she gone do it," Mamaw said, low in her throat. "She say she gone sell him away far away."

And din't it rain, my Jesus! somebody moaned.

Another simply started to cry, softly.

"Mamaaaw," Anthony cried again.

"I say to her, 'Oh, no, Missy,'" his mamaw went on, "'don't take my baby away. Don't you do that to me. Mars John, he never want you to sell my Anthony. Please, don't sell my baby. I do anythin' fer ya. Just don't do that, oh, please, Missy.'

"So she say she sell me, for Anthony. She gone send me off for two year, anyway. She movin' all us and her and everythin' to that Acquia town. And I got to go on myself someplace for two year. And she won't let me take my baby. Oh, Anthony! Who will see you all right?"

"It be hard, but don't you worry," Big Walker told her. "I watch out him like I allus do." He reached to comfort Anthony.

"Naw!" Anthony hollered, and pushed Walker's hand away.

"Anthony, hush up," Mamaw said. "He not gwoin' hurt you."

"He bein' Driver," Anthony cried.

"True, but he leader of quarry, too," Mamaw said. "He do for Mars John everythin' as long as Mars be. But Mars done gone oveh now, and Walker through bein' quarry, make him cough so. Anthony, he don't mean to pain you. What little he hurt you was to keep Mars John from painin' you more."

"Wha . . . what?" Anthony whispered.

"Walker not hurt you," Mamaw went on. "He your own great big papa, too. No more hidin' the truth. He your own paw!"

31

"Huh?"

"Mars John said you belong him, but it's a lie—I'm tellin' you so."

"Quit it, now," Big Walker said. "The boy don't have to hear all that."

"My own me don't belong to me nohow," Mamaw cried, between racking sobs. "Say who come to my bed," she moaned. "Say who sleep-a-me where. That why that Missy hate me and mine so."

"It over now," Walker said. "I ain't havin' no more no way. We gwoin' to run is what I say."

"You gwoin' to go?" All spoke at once.

"Oh, don't go. Lawd, don't go!"

"You gwoin' do that?"

"They ketch you. They do the dogs on you."

"They ain't ketch nothin'," Big Walker said. "Before we move to that Acquia, we gwoin' lose some us in these woods. She not find us, that Missy Suttle, not no her or he Mars son, Mars Charles, find us neither. Nobody ever find us." All of a sudden Walker commenced coughing so hard, he had to sit down in a corner. Someone brought him a dipper of water.

"Ain't gwoin' nowhere," Anthony whispered to Mamaw. "Me too scared of all bad wolfs."

"Huh, baby, we go where your paw wants us," Mamaw said.

"He the Big Walker. He ain't no my paw," Anthony said.

"He is—now hush."

5

MAY 25, 1854

THE WEIGHT of the past and the darkness of its night enclosed Anthony until slowly, with the growing light of day, he returned to the present.

The windows of the jury room where he was kept under guard were covered with iron bars that seemed to break the day into welts of pain. If he could somehow keep his eyes from those bright stripes, he might keep his suffering at bay. But it was no use.

Here I be! he despaired. Caught, I am, and no longer a man. Father, protect me!

He tried retreating again into the past, but all that would come to him was the time of sadness in Mamaw's cabin. With him these many years was the same question, born out of that night. "Who am I?" For the thousandth time he asked himself, "Be I the slave owner's own boy or the slave driver's son? He Mars John's or Big Walker's?"

Again, he lifted his good hand, as he had so many times before. Held it close to his eyes to see it better. There was no denying his skin was light brown. Big Walker had been a dark man, his mamaw a very black woman.

It had been whispered about the plantation that Big Walker Burns was once a freeman. That he had been tricked, caught, and brought down South. But Anthony never knew for certain if this was true, nor did any other of Mars John's black folks. Big Walker never said anything about it directly.

What matter any of it now? Anthony thought. Here I be, like a starved dog in his pen.

Anthony's stomach ached him, he was so hungry. He hadn't eaten since sometime in the dayclean before this. The room stank from the odor of stale ale and sweat. Anthony felt dizzy, then sick to his stomach from the stench. He would have to have something to eat and soon, or he would faint dead away.

Presently the heavy door to the jury room swung open. A man entered. He went over to Asa Butman. "Get him ready," he said. "We have to take him down now."

He came over to Anthony. "Deputy Marshal Riley," he said, introducing himself. "You are going to court now, Anthony. Go with Asa here. He will see that you fix yourself up a bit."

Anthony did as he was told. In a small room off to the side he washed his face and smoothed his hair. There was no comb or brush for him. He straightened his clothing. He took a tin cup of cold water that Asa offered him, but that was all he was given. When he and Butman came out again, Deputy Riley ordered irons closed around his wrists.

Anthony went numb into himself. He moved down the steps like a sleepwalker. When he entered the room set aside in this state Court House as a Federal courtroom, he made no response to seeing Colonel Suttle and William Brent there flanked by men he had never seen before— their lawyers. Also present was the one called Marshal Freeman. Some ten of his men, deputies, were with him.

Anthony took the prisoner's seat across from the judge's bench as he was directed by Asa.

"I'm makin' no promises, Tony," Colonel Suttle said to him calmly as he seated himself, "and I'm makin' no threats."

Anthony heard what Suttle said but could give no answer. He was aware of all that went on around him, but it was hard now for him to keep his mind on any one thing for long. His head felt light. He wanted so much just to lie down. The wrist irons and the chain that connected them grew heavier by the minute. Anthony couldn't find the strength or will to lift a finger even to scratch his nose, which itched him. The itching became a dull aching. It in turn spread into a throbbing loneliness throughout his body. He felt miserably hot in his shoulders and deathly cold in his legs.

Anthony bowed his head. For the rest of the time he sat as if hypnotized.

Asa Butman and one of his men took their seats on either side of Anthony. Also present and seated was the U.S. Attorney for the Federal Government, District of Massachusetts, Benjamin Hallett. Hallett was a politician who believed his position as U.S. District Attorney gave him the right to oversee the government's policy of rigidly executing the Fugitive Slave Act. He agreed with that policy, in fact. He and the other officials present hoped that the examination would be completed as soon as possible. There had been no inkling of a fugitive arrest in the morning papers. Reporters knew nothing yet about what was going on. Colonel Suttle and Mr. Brent intended to take the prisoner out of Boston and down South before the dreaded Boston "radicals" knew about his capture. Ben Hallett hoped they would, too. For if the abolitionists found out, they had a hundred ways in which they might come to Burns's defense. They might try to mob Colonel Suttle or even have him prosecuted for kidnapping.

The prisoner was definitely the slave Anthony Burns. He had admitted as much when he had first faced the colonel. It was a simple matter, then, of going through the proceeding according to law. Colonel Suttle had provided an affidavit of ownership, and Commissioner Loring had issued a warrant for Burns's arrest. There would be a hearing as soon as possible, it was hoped—all strictly according to provisions of the Fugitive Slave Act. The Commissioner would then issue the Colonel a certificate allowing him to take the prisoner back to Virginia. But unknown to the Colonel or anyone else in the courtroom, the Boston abolitionists were already informed.

Coffin Pitts, Anthony's employer and landlord, had been looking for him all the previous night.

"Anthony? Anthony!" Coffin Pitts called. When he couldn't find him anywhere in his house, he went out at once in search of him. He looked everywhere in the fugitives' quarter he could think of, but Anthony seemed to have disappeared into thin air. Fearing the worst, he went straight to Exeter Place, the home of the abolitionist Reverend Theodore Parker.

Reverend Parker was the minister of the 28th Congregational Society. He believed, he always said, in an Almighty God and the equality and dignity of all who were God's children. He had gained national attention for the sermons he preached to thousands each Sunday in the enormous music hall called Tremont Temple.

"I know that men urge in argument," Theodore Parker preached, "that the Constitution of the United States is the supreme law of the land, and that it sanctions slavery. There is no supreme law but that made by God; if our laws contradict that, the sooner they end or the sooner they are broken, why, the better."

Almost every word that Parker uttered made Coffin Pitts smile in agreement. Yet he couldn't bring himself to awaken Reverend Parker when he got to his home. He waited, nodding and dozing, on Theodore Parker's front steps all night long.

Reverend Parker found him there Thursday morning when he opened the door to let in the morning air. "Good Lord, man, come in, come in!" he said, and ushered Deacon Pitts inside. "You must be chilled through. Here, let us have coffee." Parker proceeded to the kitchen and prepared coffee while Deacon Pitts told him of the missing Anthony Burns.

"I am sorry to have to tell you this," said Parker, "but there are Virginia slavers in town."

"Oh, no!" Deacon Pitts said.

"Yes, I'm afraid so," Parker answered. "Tuesday morning

37

another colored man, a waiter from the Revere House, came to see me. Said he had waited on two Virginia slave hunters at breakfast.

"He gave me useful information," Parker continued. "The slavers are a Colonel Suttle and William Brent. But the man didn't know which slave it was they were after. So for two days I asked everyone I could think of, and nobody knew! Not even Reverend Grimes of your church— and he dared not question his congregation, lest they panic and run away north toward Canada."

Reverend Leonard Grimes had been born in Virginia of free parents who had bought their freedom from a sympathetic owner. As an adult there he ran a livery stable, and he used his horse-drawn carriages to transport fugitives farther north under cover of darkness. Once he went deep into Virginia and carried out an entire slave family; three months later he was caught and sent to prison for two years for the crime of aiding runaways. After his release Reverend Grimes moved to Boston, where he continued his work as a minister and friend to all escaped slaves.

"The slavers have been among us, hunting, and we had no wind of it for two days!" exclaimed Deacon Pitts. "They caught us unawares."

"Yes, and I daresay the slavers are here after your Anthony," replied Reverend Parker. "Well. You may stay as long as you like, Deacon Pitts, but I must be off. Have yourself another of my brew. Get yourself warmed! I'm going to the Court House."

With that, Parker hurried out. He had not let Deacon

Pitts see it, but he was seething with anger. That some men would even think to enslave other men made his blood boil. That was why, when the Fugitive Slave Act had become law in 1850, he had slapped a revolver down on his desk and left it there as clear warning to all slave hunters.

He knew that for the South, passage of the Fugitive Slave Act was a signal for an intensive manhunt in the North. And it was not long before Southern authorities sent people North to bring back fugitives and to spy on abolitionist groups. In response to this, Northern blacks and whites took direct action to head off compliance with the law. Theodore Parker found the rising tension and possibility of violence quite unpleasant. He was not a violent man himself. But if forced to, he would without question defend a fugitive with his life.

As he neared the Court House, Parker happened to meet Charles Mayo Ellis, a lawyer and member of the Boston Vigilance Committee. The Vigilance Committee was a large, secret body of abolitionists organized to operate on a moment's notice. Its main purpose was "to secure the fugitives and colored inhabitants of Boston and vicinity from any invasion of their rights."

Parker quickly explained the situation to Ellis. He then asked Ellis to go to the Court House to observe what was taking place and to keep watch over the fugitive. "I'll go find Richard Dana," Reverend Parker said. Richard Henry Dana was another member of the Vigilance Committee, a well-known novelist as well as an attorney.

But it was Reverend Leonard Grimes of the 12th Baptist

Church who was the first of the Vigilance Committee to see Anthony Burns handcuffed in the prisoner's box. Passing by the Court House, he had noticed unusual activity and had gone inside, only to see Anthony surrounded by armed guards. Alarmed, Reverend Grimes approached Anthony.

"My son, are you all right?" he asked. "Please, tell me what I may do for you now."

Anthony made no reply, and looked through space at nothing. Sadness and fear, poor soul! the reverend thought. Anthony appeared to be in a trance, unmindful or unknowing of his situation. I can't leave him alone in his condition, the reverend decided.

One of the guards at Anthony's side stood up, menacing the reverend. He put his hand on his gun butt, and Reverend Grimes backed away from the prisoner's dock. He knew it was best to act timidly before such petty officials. Quickly, bowing his head slightly, he took a seat in the rear of the court to wait and see what would happen next.

The slave catchers watched him sit down. So did District Attorney Ben Hallett. Asa Butman whispered to Hallett, "Sir, might I throw that preacher out? He ain't got any business at all bein' in here."

"No, leave him alone," Hallett said. He knew Reverend Grimes to be a respected colored minister, able enough at fund-raising to have raised ten thousand dollars and built himself a church. "Better to have him in here where we can keep an eye on him than outside where he might make trouble," he explained.

"Yassir, as you wish, then," Asa said. "But give the word and he's out as quick as you please." He winked at Hallett as if they were conspirators.

Ben Hallett looked pained. To think he must depend on the lowest life, such as Butman, to see that the Federal law was enforced! He turned away in distaste and busied himself with his court papers as Asa hurried back to his post beside Anthony.

6

MAY 25, 1854

RICHARD HENRY DANA was not in his office when Theodore Parker went there looking for him. He had learned early that morning, as had Reverend Grimes, that a fugitive was about to appear in court before Commissioner Edward G. Loring. While passing the Court House on his way to work, Dana had been approached by a stranger and told the bad news.

"Good God!" he had said. "I need a runner!" He soon found a Negro youth he knew well, one of the many among the growing community of free persons and fugitives who lived in Boston.

Without further delay Dana sent the youth to find members of the Boston Vigilance Committee. For it was the Committee's sworn duty to defend, without fee, all black inhabitants of Boston and vicinity against slavers and bounty hunters.

Dana, one of the Committee's most illustrious members, had helped defend the fugitive slave Thomas Sims in court in 1851. As a young man he had withdrawn from

Harvard when measles had weakened his eyesight, and had, in 1834, shipped out to California as a sailor to regain his health. After calling at California's ports loading cargo, his ship sailed around Cape Horn and returned home to Boston in 1835.

Dana's travel experiences cured him physically and also taught him sympathy for the less fortunate. He reentered Harvard and was admitted to the Massachusetts bar in 1840. That same year he published *Two Years Before the Mast*, a novel written from diaries he'd kept at sea about "the life of a common sailor as it really is." In it he revealed the awful abuses endured by his fellow seamen at the hands of their superiors. The book made him famous.

When the slavery question moved North with the fugitives, Dana put novel writing aside. His political party was Free Soil, which meant he did not oppose slavery in the South. But he vowed to fight against its spread into the western land tracts, such as Kansas and Nebraska. He lost many of his wealthy, proslavery clients because of this "moderate" view, but he didn't care.

"I am against slavery in the North," he said again and again.

By 1854 Dana no longer put much faith in justice. He had defended two slaves already, Sims and another popularly known as Shadrach, and neither case had ended well. Sims had lost his case and was returned to Georgia, where he died. Shadrach had been "stolen," from the very Court House that now held Anthony Burns, by black abolitionists who managed to get him away to freedom.

Justice and law both had come out scarred and battered, Dana observed grimly at the time. But he believed that gentlemen must behave with justice. And if slave hunters wished to take back a slave, then they would have to proceed at every turn strictly according to the law.

Let them make a single wrong explanation, and I will have them! Richard Dana thought.

Now he braced himself and entered the courtroom.

Dana swiftly took in the scene, observing the armed guards around the prisoner. So that's Burns, he thought. And as pitiful-looking a fugitive as I've ever seen. Not the man Sims was, surely. This one looks lost witted.

The slave had a small scar on his cheek—a brand of some kind, Dana supposed. One hand, his right, was hideously deformed, and Dana assumed at once that Burns had been awfully mistreated by his owner. He glanced over at the man within the bar—the railing that separated the public from the rest of the courtroom—who he rightly guessed was Colonel Charles Suttle, slave owner of Virginia, surrounded by his agent and lawyers.

So then, Dana thought, they mean to have it all their way, and quickly. But not so fast!

He walked over to Anthony, ignoring the guards and Marshal Freeman. "I'm a lawyer," he said to Anthony. "Richard Dana is my name. Let me help you. And there will be no fee."

Anthony was shocked to hear the learned voice of a white man speaking to him. Who? . . . A buckra again. Seems to care . . . kind voice. But the Colonel, he standing up. Glaring so at me.

Colonel Suttle, hearing what Dana had said, had risen to his feet. His face was red with fury.

Anthony dared not answer Richard Dana.

"Anthony," Dana persisted, "there are certain papers from Virginia that an owner must have in order. These might have mistakes. And you might get off if you have a lawyer."

There was a long silence. Anthony was thinking, Oh, I feel so ashamed. I should have said something to Reverend Grimes first, when Mr. Grimes come to talk to me. Should have said how sorry I was to have got myself captured. How I should've gone to the dedication of Reverend Grimes' church. Then maybe none of this would have happened.

Oh, so many shoulds!

The white man still stood there before him.

"I . . . I . . ." Anthony began.

"Yes?" Dana said quickly.

"I . . . don't know," Anthony finished, murmuring so low that Dana had to come even closer to hear.

Anthony didn't know what to do. He did know that Mars Charles would make his life miserable if it cost him extra time and money to get Anthony back down South.

"Anthony? Tell me what you want," Dana said.

"It's of no use," Anthony responded, finally. "They know me. Mars Charles, the Colonel, knows me. I will fare worse if I resist."

Dana straightened up. He reasoned that Anthony was frightened out of his wits by the numbers of hostile white men in the room—a dozen guards, all armed, the Marshal, the District Attorney, his owner, and the others. Clearly, Anthony was threatened by them.

I can't defend him unless he wants me to, Dana kept

thinking. The fugitive must ask to be represented. Dana could not otherwise take his case. I need time! he was thinking.

At that instant four other abolitionist lawyers, members of the Vigilance Committee, entered the court: Charles Mayo Ellis, Theodore Parker, Wendell Phillips, and a black lawyer, Robert Morriss.

Not two minutes later the Commissioner, Judge Edward Loring, walked briskly in.

Immediately, Marshal Freeman spoke loudly, "The court. All rise."

Anthony was made to stand, as everyone in the courtroom got to his feet. After the judge sat down, Anthony and the rest sat.

Judge Loring looked askance at all the guards in the room. He asked Marshal Freeman why there were so many and was told how difficult were the circumstances surrounding the capture of Burns. Judge Loring then asked whether the defendant was in the prisoner's dock.

"Yes, Your Honor," the Marshal answered.

"Is the claimant here, or his agent?" Loring asked.

"Both of them are here, Judge," Marshal Freeman answered.

"Then we may begin," Judge Loring said.

At that point Richard Dana asked to speak to Loring privately.

Loring agreed, and Dana explained how frightened the prisoner, Anthony Burns, was. "He cannot act even in his own behalf," Dana said. "I suggest that you call him up to the bench instead of addressing him in the prisoner's dock. He will then be out of the way of the gaze of the claimant, Colonel Suttle. And so we might know what he wants to do."

"I intend to do that," Judge Loring said. "But now I must proceed."

"Yes, of course," Dana said, "thank you, Your Honor." And he sat down.

Judge Loring started the proceedings by saying that he was presiding as a U.S. Commissioner, that his duties were executive, and that the hearing was an inquiry. The question before the court, he said, was whether he should award to Charles F. Suttle a certificate authorizing him to take to Virginia the slave Anthony Burns. The claim was that Anthony Burns owed Mr. Suttle service and labor.

"There are three facts that are to be proved," Loring said. "And these are: that Anthony Burns escaped from slavery from the state of Virginia; that Anthony Burns was by the law of Virginia the slave of Charles F. Suttle; that the prisoner is indeed Anthony Burns.

"If counsel for Charles Suttle can prove these facts," the judge continued, "I am empowered to issue a certificate stating the proofs; this will allow the rendition of Anthony Burns."

Anthony listened now and understood. He knew what rendition was. Means me, he thought, taken back home by Mars Charles. Means me, a slave again.

He swallowed hard and felt himself retreat within. But there was no comfort now. His loneliness and fear, his wretched hunger, wouldn't permit him to bring the memory of Mamaw into this harsh place. Neither could he bring forth the child he had been. Where was that young Anthony now? he wondered, for he could not summon the image of the boy he had been.

The second counsel for Charles Suttle, Edward G. Parker, now rose, and read from the warrant for Anthony's arrest:

"In the name of the President of the United States of America, you are hereby commanded forthwith to apprehend Anthony Burns, a negro man, alleged now to be in your District, charged with being a fugitive from labor, and with having escaped from service in the State of Virginia, and have him forthwith before me, Edward G. Loring, one of the Commissioners of the Circuit Court of the United States, there to answer to the complaint of Charles F. Suttle, of Alexandria, alleging under oath that said Burns, on the twenty-fourth day of March last, and for a long time prior thereto had owed service and labor to him in the State of Virginia and that, while held to service there by said Suttle, the said Burns escaped into the said State of Massachusetts. . . ."

He next read the record of the Virginia Court as required by the Fugitive Slave Act:

"In Alexandria Circuit Court, May 16, 1854. On the application of Charles F. Suttle, who this day appeared in Court and made satisfactory proof to the Court that Anthony Burns was held to service and labor by him in the State of Virginia, and service and labor are due to him from the said Anthony, and that the said Anthony has

*escaped. Anthony is a man of dark complexion, about six
feet high, with a scar on one of his cheeks, and also a scar
on the back of his right hand, and about twenty-three or
four years of age—it is therefore ordered, in pursuance of
an act of Congress, 'An Act respecting Fugitives from Justice and Persons escaping from the Service of their masters,' that the matter set forth be entered on the record of .
this Court."*

The abolitionist lawyer Charles Mayo Ellis watched the
proceedings closely. When he saw Richard Dana speak
privately to Judge Loring, he supposed Dana meant to
make himself the lawyer for Anthony Burns. But when
this did not seem to be his purpose, Mr. Ellis made his
way to Dana's side as quietly as he could.

As Edward Parker went on with the Alexandria Circuit
Court record, Ellis spoke urgently to Richard Dana.
"Loring is sitting as a *judge*, Richard. You must *do* something. Massachusetts law clearly forbids judges sitting on
slave cases.

"There's no jury," Ellis added. "The armed guards sitting illegally in the jury box are plainly petty thieves being
used to terrify an already frightened man."

Richard Dana shrugged. "What can I do?" he said.
"Anthony Burns would seem to want to go back without
trouble to his master. He won't accept my aid."

Reverend Theodore Parker got to his feet. He could
stand it no longer. It was clear to him that the poor fugitive was being tried without a lawyer. He marched angrily
to the front of the courtroom just as Edward Parker was
finishing and before Marshal Freeman could testify.

49

He strode up to the witness box and peered into it. On seeing that Anthony was handcuffed, he glared indignantly at Judge Loring. Next, he spoke to Anthony.

"I am Theodore Parker," he said. "I am a minister. Surely you want me to help you."

He could see that Anthony was frozen with fear. "Let us give you counsel," Parker said. "Richard Dana there is the best lawyer in Boston. He is on your side! The black man over there is Robert Morriss and a fine lawyer, too. Will you not let us defend you?"

Anthony began to shake all over. Lord, oh, Lord! Tell me what I must do! he thought.

But he couldn't help seeing that Mars Charles Suttle watched him, that Mars Brent watched him. Anthony commenced stammering, "Mars . . . Mars . . . Colonel . . . he know . . . he knows me . . . I shall have to go back. Mars Brent . . . know me."

"But it can do you no harm to make a defense," urged Parker.

"I shall have to go back," Anthony said again. "If I must . . . go back, I want ter go back as easy as I can—but—do as you have a mind to."

Theodore Parker strode back to his seat. He was thinking that if Charles Suttle's lawyers put a nervous witness on the stand and the witness made a false statement, they might have a case. He gave a nod to Richard Dana, to say that Dana had the prisoner's permission to defend him.

Colonel Suttle's other lawyer, Seth Thomas, now rose. He was upset that Theodore Parker had interrupted, but he did not show it. He at once put William Brent upon the stand as a witness to prove the identity of the prisoner with the person named in the arrest warrant. Brent gave his testimony confidently.

He was a merchant from Richmond, Virginia, he said. And he was a close friend of Colonel Suttle.

"Do you know Anthony Burns?" Mr. Thomas asked.

"Yes, I know him well," he said. And he stated that Anthony Burns was the prisoner in the prisoner's box.

"Can you tell us something about Anthony Burns?" Thomas asked.

Brent began speaking as if reciting: "Anthony Burns was owned by the Colonel's mother. Colonel Suttle has owned him for some fourteen years. I paid the Colonel for the services of Anthony Burns in 1846, '47, and '48."

"Good. Now then," the lawyer said, "can you tell me what you know about his escape?"

"In March," said Brent, "Anthony was missing from Richmond. I didn't see him again until last day past, when he spoke to his master."

"Kindly repeat what was said then," said Thomas.

Theodore Parker rose to his feet again. Brent's statements concerning this conversation would be improper testimony. "You've got to defend him now," he told Richard Dana as he stood. "And if you won't, I will!"

Judge Loring struck with his gavel in an effort to quiet Reverend Parker. Before the Marshal and his deputies could think to restrain the pastor, Richard Dana rose to address the court. It was clear to him that the prisoner would have to have his aid at once. Under the Fugitive

Slave Act, the testimony of the alleged fugitive could not be admitted as evidence. Despite this, Anthony's testimony was about to be admitted. Dana had to prevent this.

He presented himself to Judge Loring as *amicus curiae*, or friend of the court—one who is called in to advise the court. "I urge Your Honor that there be a delay so that the prisoner can decide what would be his best course," he said.

"I oppose this motion, Your Honor," responded Seth Thomas. "The prisoner by his own statement has admitted that he is Charles Suttle's slave. He does not want a lawyer, nor does he want a defense."

"The prisoner is in no condition to determine whether he would have counsel or not!" Dana said heatedly. "He does not know what he is saying. He must be given time to recover himself and to talk with a lawyer."

Over the objections of both of Suttle's lawyers, Judge Loring had Anthony Burns brought before him. Marshal Freeman hurriedly unlocked Anthony's wrist irons before leading him to the judge.

Loring spoke to Anthony in a kindly manner, explaining what the claim against him was. "Anthony, do you wish to make a defense to this claim?" he asked. "If you do, you can have counsel to aid you, and you shall have time to make a defense. You have a right to a defense if you wish for one."

Anthony finally dared look around the room slowly. His gaze rested on Richard Dana and then on Robert Morriss, but he made no reply.

Dana thought it was all over then. But Judge Loring

said to Anthony reassuringly. "Anthony, do you wish for time to think about this? Do you wish to go away and meet me here tomorrow or next day, and tell me what you will do?"

All in the courtroom watched Anthony. He gave a slight twitching of his deformed hand, but no one knew whether he meant yes or no by the movement. He did not know himself.

I will have to go back, he was thinking. I will be whipped unto an inch of my life. I will die a slave.

Judge Loring looked doubtful, but at last he said to Anthony, "I understand you to say that you would."

Very faintly, Anthony said, "I would."

"Then you shall have it," Loring said.

Marshal Freeman whispered to the judge. Judge Loring replied out loud, "No sir, he must have the time necessary."

Again the Marshal whispered. Judge Loring replied sternly, "I can't help that, sir—he shall have the proper time."

The day was Thursday. "You shall have until Saturday morning," Judge Loring told Anthony and his defenders, and struck his gavel down.

Anthony was taken back to the jury room high up in the court building. There four men, including Deputy Asa Butman, guarded him.

"Tony, boy," Butman said to him, mimicking words spoken by Charles Suttle, "now we here are curious. Did the Colonel just *raise* you up or did he *buy* you from somebody?"

53

The other guards nodded encouragement. "Come on, lad, you know us here for your friends."

Anthony knew they thought him a fool. He had figured out that they hoped to get information from him for Mars Charles and Mars Brent. He knew there must be a reward for him. Every runaway slave had a price on his head.

Wonder how much Mars Charles think me worth?

Anthony played dumb; he acted confused, stared off into space, and told his jailers nothing.

THE COURT had emptied, and almost at once news of Anthony's arrest spread throughout Boston. The concerned public learned that slave hunters were in the city, hoping to force another wretched soul back into bondage.

All sympathetic citizens, and there were thousands, felt duty bound to disobey the Fugitive Slave act on behalf of the captured fugitive in their midst. But there was another factor that mobilized them: for months there had been a proposal before Congress that would allow slavery in the Great Plains lands of Kansas and Nebraska. The two tracts were to be territories within the Louisiana Purchase, the enormous parcel of land, stretching from the Gulf of Mexico to Canada, bought from France in 1803. The Missouri Compromise of 1820 had closed the Louisiana Purchase to slavery "forever." But people on the proslavery as well as the antislavery sides had been sending their settlers into Kansas and Nebraska to agitate and to be in a position to vote for their sides once the territories were divided into states.

On May 25, 1854, the very same day that Anthony

appeared in court, the Kansas-Nebraska Bill passed in the United States Senate. It permitted slavery in states that would be carved from the two territories if it was provided for in the state constitutions. So in effect it repealed the Missouri Compromise. After these victories for slavery, the jailing of a poor fugitive in a Boston court house at the bidding of a slave owner was the very last straw for those against slavery. Thus had the slavocracy rocked the cradle of liberty.

By evening the news that Anthony Burns had escaped from the South only to be captured in the free North moved from town to town and newspaper to newspaper across the country.

KIDNAPPING AGAIN! read the first leaflet out of Boston that told the tale:

A man was stolen Last Night
By the Fugitive Slave Bill Commissioner
He will have His

MOCK
TRIAL

On Saturday, May 27, in the Kidnapper's Court
Before the Honorable Slave Bill Commissioner
At the Court House in Court Square

SHALL BOSTON STEAL ANOTHER MAN?

Thursday, May 25, 1854

Written by Reverend Parker, the leaflet was printed by the antislavery press and carried across Massachusetts by volunteers who worked on trains, stagecoaches, and trucks. As it was being distributed, Theodore Parker had time to fire off another leaflet:

SEE TO IT THAT NO FREE CITIZEN OF MASSACHUSETTS
IS DRAGGED INTO SLAVERY

Overnight, without his ever knowing it, Anthony Burns became a symbol of freedom. But high up in the Court House he was a tired, miserable prisoner, alone save for his guard of petty criminals.

Anthony felt he had no one to turn to. He had no way of knowing that all through the night men watched the three massive doors of his granite prison Court House. It was a different time from 1851, when Thomas Sims was taken. The watchers made certain the authorities knew of their presence. Their message was clear: Anthony Burns was cared for.

Anthony was unaware that abolitionist ministers and lawyers argued fiercely hour upon hour over their next course of action on his behalf. There was no one to inform him that the slavers, Suttle and Brent, were followed everywhere by black men who never looked at them but were always in their sight. Suttle became so terrified that these blacks would try to lynch him, he and Brent moved to quarters in the Revere House attic and hired body-guards.

In two short days Anthony had become a symbol to freedom lovers and a devilish token of danger to slavers like Suttle. But the courteous Reverend Leonard Grimes and his deacon, Coffin Pitts, never for an instant confused the man, the fugitive, with his cause. They agreed that Reverend Grimes must try to see Anthony the next morning.

Anthony knew none of this. He wished to shut out the prying questions of guards hoping to trick him. He did what he knew how to do best of all: He retreated within, taking comfort in his unchanging past.

7

WINTER 1846

THE BOY of his past was now twelve. At that time he had just finished two years' service to Mars William and Missy Brent in Falmouth, Virginia.

"I be two year with Brents," spoke the boy. "Missy treat me kind, and all 'em be house slaves she treat the same. She let me read secret in her house. And I gain two hundred money for Mars Brent. He hired me out and I done it all well."

Charles Suttle had more black slaves then he could possibly need or use. He had mortgaged his land and sold much of it to pay off past debts. By the time Anthony was grown, Suttle was a shopkeeper and a high sheriff. In his part of Virginia, Stafford County, the land had been worked almost to death. So Suttle began to hire out his slaves to people who had none and needed workers. It became so profitable for him to supply other towns and cities that he made more of his women slaves into breeders to keep up the supply of slave labor.

When Anthony came back to the Suttle home after his second year with the Brents, Suttle said, "Tony, Mr. Brent speaks very well of you. Likes you so well, he has hired you for another year."

"But Mars Charles, I haven't hire *him*," Anthony said. He was confident he could speak boldly to his owner, for he knew Mars Charles favored him.

"What's the matter, boy—hasn't Brent treated you well?" asked Suttle.

"Well, yes, Mars, but there's th'tuther boy there mislikes me, and—"

Suttle shook his head. "It can't be helped now," he said. "I've agreed to let you stop with Mr. Brent. And besides, he pays more for you this year than he did last year."

"Just as you say, Mars. The *woods* is big enough to hold *me*," Anthony said.

Charles Suttle was surprised. This was the first time Anthony had used the *argument of the woods*, and it was a position that carried weight with every slaveholder. So much of Virginia was dense forest that a slave might disappear into the deep woods of Stafford County and run for weeks under cover clear to the North. In Anthony's case it meant that if Suttle did not consider what he wanted, Anthony might run away into the forest, where it would be difficult to catch him again. If word got around that Anthony had raised the *argument*, it would lower his value. For no one wanted to hire or purchase a slave with the runaway disease.

Suttle sighed. "All right, Tony," he said. "This time I'll let you have it your way."

Anthony's heart sprang for joy. He could leave Mars Brent!

"But you must now repair to the Hiring Ground," Suttle told him. "And you will lead some of my Jims. Take Efrum, and Luther, Simon, and Whittom.

"You are in charge," Suttle added. "You know how to go."

"Yay sur, I know," Anthony said, for he had hired out before. The Hiring Ground was in Stafford County, in a large village of more than two hundred houses, fifteen miles along the river. Its exact location was by the market and near the court house. It was in no way hard to find. Thinking about it gave Anthony mixed feelings, both somber and pleasant. He knew that if he could keep moving, he might find a way to freedom. Mamaw had told him all about it. Freedom was north. "Go find it," she had said. The Hiring Ground might bring him one step closer.

"You meet me there with my Jims tomorry," Suttle said. "Here is money for their food."

"I would have a penny for my lodging," Anthony boldly said.

Suttle looked at him sternly. "I ought to slap you in the face for that," he said. "You will sleep with the rest, Tony. How can you keep your eye on them if you are not beside them? And if they get into difficulty, you will pay me for it."

"Yay sur," Anthony mumbled, bowing his head as was proper. This time he had gone too far, but there was always hope in trying. He would ever try to get his way, forcing his owner to give a little and a little more each time. It was a small opening of freedom's door.

By seven o'clock the next morning, Anthony was ready. He gathered his charges and saw to it that they were dressed carefully enough for the hiring time. He gave them their passes, which allowed them to leave the Suttle house and their village and enter the next village for the purpose stated by their owner.

"Now don't you lose 'em papers," he said, " 'cause Mars Suttle won't be comin' till middayclean. We on my own time till then. And I ain't having no pateroller along the way saying how we running so's he can sell us off to Loozanna."

Anthony watched as each lad put his pass away in his clothing. "You get a little bread, a little cracklin'," he said, and handed some to each. He carried a gourd for water. One of the others did also.

Soon they were on their way. Anthony kept an even, fairly fast pace. So much so that after the food was eaten, he had to cajole his group along.

"Too quick, Anthony," Whittom said. He was a hangback youth, even in this cool winter weather.

"Keep you warmer, walking fast," Anthony told him.

"Then talk some more," Whittom panted.

"I am talking," Anthony said, and began a quiz. "Who's oldest of Mars Charles' black folks?"

61

They all answered promptly. "Your own mama!"

"That's it," Anthony said. "And who's youngest of Mars Eldy's colored boys?"

They all thought about the nearest planter's young male slaves. They saw other planters and their slaves only at church-sermon time. "That be one they calls By Big Ducey," said Whittom.

"But what his name called?" asked Anthony.

"That be the name!" cried Efrum.

"That just be who 'em by," Luther said. "I know what his name called."

"Then tell," said Anthony.

"You know?" Luther asked him.

"Course I do."

"Then you tell it."

Anthony almost did when he realized he was being tricked. It wouldn't do for Mars Charles to learn that one of his own boys had beaten Anthony. Luther wanted to be leader someday soon, Anthony knew. Not this soon! he thought.

"It my quiz," Anthony told him.

"Well," Luther said, "if I got to. It one they call Little Henry. Ain't but one Christmas old."

"He right?" Whittom ask.

"He right," Anthony said. "Somebody else tell something. I'm tired."

"I got something," Simon said.

"Say it, then," Anthony told him.

"Hear tell." It was the way a story began.

"Then tell," the others replied.

62

"Hear tell the pot call the skillet black."

"We all know that the pot call the skillet black." Whittom laughed.

"But you don't know what in the skillet when pot call him black."

"Huh?" Luther said.

Anthony chuckled. "Tell it, Simon."

"Grease," Simon said. "And Bruh Rabbit be lying in the skillet grease."

"No!" everyone said.

"Didn't I just say so?" Simon said.

"What that rabbit doing in there?" Anthony wanted to know.

"He doing grease-to-fry labor," Simon said. "He doing up *brown*. He got one back leg cooked brown clear to his thighbone. The other back foot be hanging over the rim and still raw. And Bruh Rabbit holler his head off, too, and clappin' his front paws in time with the holler.

" 'You black thang thar,' call the cook pot hanging on the wall," Simon said. " 'Can't ya keep that beast-um quiet?' Well, skillet get so mad, pot callin' him black, that he thew the grease up the wall, trying to catch that pot. 'Shew!' skillet call to pot. 'You black youself, so hesh up!' Well. That grease hot-splatter every which-a-way. And rabbit, he fall to the floor. He skidaddle on him three good legs outta there. I saw him last month, sittin' on a stump. Say to him," Simon said, " 'Bruh, you got a leg up and what for?' 'Cause rabbit holding his leg up like it still sore. And rabbit say to me, 'Pot call skillet black. 'Cause guess she be thinkin' she white.' "

They had stopped in the dusty way. They surrounded Simon, watching his eyes. "Took me a month a Sunday's to find out what for Bruh Rabbit fry he leg up."

Simon looked off into the distance, like he could see something standing on thin, cool air. When they followed his gaze, he tricked them, as quick as you please: "And-I-ain't-lyin'!" Simon said.

They roared with laughter. There was something about saying the ending when they least expected it that always made them hold back their laughter until that point. Because in the tell, Rabbit would answer one question and keep from answering another. And so would Simon.

"So that's why the pot call the skillet black," Anthony said. " 'Cause *she* think she white." He shook his head, grinning.

"And Skillet be a black folk! And a *she*, too!" Efrum said, laughing.

"Heard tell it," Simon said simply.

"Wonder why that rabbit in that grease skillet first place," Anthony said. He eyed Simon.

Simon looked a way off, a faint smile on his face. "Said he'd tell me next time," Simon said.

Anthony gave him an affectionate shove. He almost knocked Simon over. "Ooops," Anthony said. "Didn't mean to hurt you."

"Didn't hurt me," Simon said.

But he was small and wiry, on the frail side. Anthony reminded himself to be careful with him.

Probably why Simon liked to tell about rabbit so much,

he thought. Rabbit was small, but he was also smart. Just like Simon.

There were sure to be other pot-'n'-skillet and rabbit tells.

They set off again for the Hiring Ground. They moved at a good pace, but more slowly, as though some of the fun were leaving them. And it was true, as they drew nearer to the Ground, that Anthony left off talking and his face grew serious. Most of the time he kept his eyes fixed on his moving feet.

Thus did Anthony spend his second night in jail, as if in a stupor, yet within reliving a vivid time of his past.

8

MAY 26, 1854

WHEN THE fugitive Thomas Sims was captured and returned to slavery in 1851, five hundred business and
professional men of Boston volunteered as special consta-
bles to aid Marshal Freeman in removing the prisoner
from the city. But public sentiment had changed so greatly
by the year 1854 that now no decent man would help the
Marshal serve up another slave. Harriet Beecher Stowe's
Uncle Tom's Cabin, published in 1852, had become an
immense success. The book had created broad sympathy
for the plight of slaves, and in the North it had stirred
antislavery emotions to a high pitch. It also primed the
growing territorial disputes.

With the passage of the Kansas-Nebraska Bill of 1854,
Kansas was sure to seek admission to the Union as a
slave state and Nebraska as a free state. Free-state com-
munities and secret slavery societies were formed and
settled in Kansas, bringing violence and bloodshed and
civil war. "Bleeding Kansas" became the rallying cry for
both sides in the bitter battle.

Freedom lovers in the North were more deeply concerned and more determined than ever to resist the Fugitive Slave Act. They feared that if slavery could enter the territories, it could slither just as easily into the free states of the North. The Vigilance Committee, determined to forestall this at any cost, worked in secret against the law and the government to aid fugitive slaves.

Friday morning, the day after Anthony stood before the Commissioner, Richard Dana tried to get him released from jail until Saturday, when he was to appear in court again. But Commissioner Loring refused to allow this. Privately Loring had told the abolitionist Wendell Phillips that he thought the case was clear, that Burns would probably have to go back to where he came from.

A little later on Friday, Dana went to the Court House with Reverend Grimes. They did not speak much. Richard Dana was deep in thought, and the reverend appeared to have some thinking of his own to do.

It was indeed a sorry business, thought Dana, if Edward Loring had prejudged the case. Massachusetts law of 1843, passed by a state legislature determined not to go along with earlier Federal laws regarding runaway slaves, forbade state officers and magistrates to assist in the business of returning fugitives. The terms of this law also included judges of probate; Edward Loring was just such a judge as well as United States Commissioner. Why hadn't a gentleman of such respectability resigned his commission rather than carry out the Fugitive Slave Act? Dana could only guess that Loring, by acting upon the slave law, supported President Franklin Pierce, whose administration was decidedly proslavery.

Wendell Phillips had told Dana that Edward Loring

thought the Burns case was clearly on the side of Colonel Suttle, and that he believed Anthony would go back to Virginia. Dana didn't think Loring had meant harm to the defense. He wouldn't use Loring's words against him in court. The conversation had to be regarded as a private one between one gentleman and another.

The Judge can meet any argument we might raise on the constitutionality of the Fugitive Slave Act itself, Dana was thinking; the act has already been upheld in higher courts.

But the claimant, Suttle, is trying to prove too much. Not only the prisoner's identity, but that he escaped as well. And there is no clear evidence of that. If Burns fell asleep on the ship, then clearly he did not escape. And if he did not escape, then he cannot be the "escaped slave" of their record. The person described in the record would have to be someone other than Anthony Burns.

Dana stayed only briefly with the prisoner, to tell Anthony that he would represent him. He found Burns to be a man self-possessed now, not like the frightened creature in Thursday's courtroom. He took Anthony to one of the windows and quietly explained again who he was and that he would take care of the business in court for him. All the time he was thinking that Anthony seemed a pleasant fellow and quite intelligent.

Good! Dana thought. He can think for himself; he can read and write. And he therefore can help us defend him. Very good!

Reverend Grimes also had his mind on Anthony. How would he find Mr. Burns this day? he wondered. How was a man once free going to bear being confined again? Some men would become wild and raging. Others would quickly die inside, forever broken in heart and mind. Would that be the state of Anthony Burns?

Mr. Grimes waited calmly outside for his turn to see Anthony. When he entered the jury room, he found that Anthony was dictating a letter to one of his jailers. Anthony had written some few words of it himself, proud to show he could write.

Reverend Grimes greeted Anthony warmly. "What have you been doing with yourself, Mr. Burns?" he asked.

Anthony told the reverend, "This fellow here says the Boston people think on how the Colonel has been awful hard with me. The Colonel, Mars Suttle, don't like that at all. Well, this man says if I straight it out, then the Colonel is not going to make it bad for me when I get back. So that be what I had writ down here for all to see."

Reverend Grimes was shocked. Obviously the guard had been instructed to trick Anthony and to get him to make admissions to be used in court.

The poor soul's mind is weakened by this confinement, Mr. Grimes thought. "I will get Mr. Dana back here," he told the guard. "Sir, I will get *all* of Mr. Burns's lawyers here. Sir, you will bring trouble unto yourself for this!"

This last was said with such force and in such a tone that the guard stepped back, stammering an apology. He took the letter, dictated and carefully signed by Anthony Burns, and quickly handed it to Asa Butman.

"Mr. Burns," Reverend Grimes whispered urgently, "you must get that letter back. They mean to use it against you!"

Anthony was shaken. Suddenly he knew he had been

a fool. "Don't know what has got inside me," he said. "Must be the Devil's own self. Don't know what I'm about. They always try to trick me. And I let them do it. All this—prison confuse me so. I do forget even what day— I'll get that letter back! I will!"

"I know you will do it," Reverend Grimes said, "just as I am sure the lawyers will get you off. Mr. Ellis and Mr. Dana are both fine men. And all of our group here are going to see that no one harms you or takes you back."

"Thank you all!" Anthony said, smiling. He did not show it, but he was not convinced he would go free. He was used to the power of the slave owners. Their strength had been tested and was a fact of life for him even now.

It always been so, he thought. Ain't the colonel found me clear to here? No changing what be the truth. Mars Charles will win me.

There was no way for the reverend to know how forlorn Anthony felt. He would not have guessed that when the guards left him to himself, Anthony would go far back in his mind to slavery times for comfort. And even if Mr. Grimes had known, he wouldn't have believed such solace could be found in dark bondage. But Anthony was no ordinary fugitive. And he took his comfort where he could.

Soon Reverend Grimes had to say good-bye to Anthony. "You will remember to get the letter, my son?" he said.

"Oh, surely, I will get it," Anthony said. "I will."

Anthony did get it back. Later that morning, after Reverend Grimes had gone, he got the letter back under the pretext of wanting to add something to it. Once he had the letter in his hands, Anthony tore it to shreds instantly. Asa Butman looked like he could have shot Anthony on the spot. But he did nothing.

After the guards left him to himself, Anthony stood a long time at one of the windows. He gripped the bars, pressing his head up against the iron stripes. Get it over, he thought. Lord? Good Lord. I can't take much more.

Few men ever had felt so alone as Anthony did at that moment. But he was not alone. Some members of the secret Vigilance Committee stayed with him, watching over the Court House exits as long as he was there. Others kept a sharp eye on the slave owners at the Revere House. Night and day Colonel Suttle and William Brent's steps were dogged by black men who moved like shadows. When the slaveholders had been followed by one dark, silent figure for a certain length of time, they were passed along to another and still another. At no time were the two Virginians ever left alone in public. It was no wonder then that Colonel Suttle and William Brent kept to their attic rooms as much as possible.

The Vigilance Committee had at its command lawyers, scholars, doctors, suffragettes, and ship captains as well as working men and women both black and white. All were dedicated to the cause of freedom for slaves.

The leaders of the Committee met secretly late Friday afternoon, May 26, in Theodore Parker's church, Tremont Temple. They had already obtained permission to hold a protest meeting at Faneuil Hall that evening. Posters announcing the evening meeting were up all over Boston. A notice appeared in all the papers Friday morning:

A MAN KIDNAPPED—*A Public Meeting will be held at Faneuil Hall this evening, May 26, at 7 o'clock, to secure justice for a man claimed as a slave by a Virginia kidnapper, and imprisoned in Boston Court House, in defiance of the laws of Massachusetts. Shall he be plunged into the hell of a Virginia slavery by a Massachusetts Judge of Probate?*

Letters to important abolitionists and Vigilance Committee members in western and southern Massachusetts were carried out of the city by teamsters, men who drove their wagons of vegetables and fish to market Thursday night.

That Friday afternoon at Parker's church, the Committee decided that Anthony Burns would never be taken back to Virginia, no matter what Judge Loring's decision might be. It decided that if any attempt was made to remove the prisoner back to the South, a wall of men would bar the way. In the confusion that would then result, the Committee men would hustle Anthony into a waiting carriage and on to safety.

There were other ideas about how to proceed. Some members wanted to attack the Court House and rescue Anthony by the use of force, just as the slave Shadrach had been liberated in 1851. Others felt that they should wait for Loring's decision. If the decision went against Anthony, then they proposed to take to the streets. If Burns was escorted out of the Court House to be taken to Virginia, they would start a riot. And as with the first plan, in the confusion, they would grab Anthony Burns and escape. But after long hours of discussion, no definite course of

72

action was decided at the meeting, and it adjourned with only vague notions of resistance.

Reverend Thomas W. Higginson of Worcester, Massachusetts, had attended the Parker church meeting after receiving a call-to-meeting letter from a Boston teamster the day before. Higginson's own church was a strong force in Worcester; he had also been involved in the Sims case of 1851. Eager to help, he took a train to Boston on Friday with more than two hundred Worcester citizens. Displeased with the outcome of the meeting at Parker's church, Higginson met with another Worcester man, Martin Stowell, afterward. They formed their own secret plan.

The two of them believed that Anthony Burns *must* be taken from the Court House by sympathizers, who could carry him off during the excitement of a public meeting like the one that was to take place at Faneuil Hall that very night. Reverend Higginson was certain that Marshal Freeman would be expecting such an attack at the end of the Faneuil Hall meeting.

"Could there not be an attack at the very *height* of the meeting?" he asked. "Let all be in readiness; let a picked body be distributed near the Court House and Square; then send some loud-voiced speaker, who should appear in the gallery of Faneuil Hall and announce that there was a mob of Negroes already attacking. Let a speaker, previously warned, accept the opportunity promptly and send the whole meeting to Court Square, ready to fall behind the leaders and bring out the slave."

That, then, was their plan—the rescue of Anthony Burns from the Court House. Higginson and Stowell separated to inform the men they would need to carry it out.

9

MAY 26, 1854

A FEW HOURS later, at seven that evening, Faneuil Hall was filled to overflowing. The call to duty and honor had gone out, and freedom lovers from all over New England had responded. The audience, more than 2,000 strong, was demanding and confident, ready for action if not outright riot. Newspapers that day stated that the interest in the fugitive slave was "only general." But the huge size of the crowd proved otherwise.

The evening had been organized as a public meeting. Presiding was George R. Russell, from the neighboring city of Roxbury and formerly that city's mayor. He delivered his opening remarks in a voice dripping with sarcasm: "I once thought that a fugitive could never be taken from Boston. I was mistaken! The time will come when slavery will pass away, and our children shall have only its hideous memory to make them wonder at the deeds of their fathers. For one I hope to die in a land of liberty—in a land which no slave hunter shall dare pollute with his presence."

Wild applause splintered the air. It died only when the next speaker took center stage.

Dr. Samuel G. Howe was a philanthropist and historian whose abolitionist/suffragette wife, Julia Ward Howe, was to write "The Battle Hymn of the Republic." He next presented a series of resolutions that expressed the opinions of nearly all who were present:

"The time has come to declare and demonstrate that no slave hunter can carry his prey from the Commonwealth of Massachusetts. That which is not just is not law, and that which is not law ought not to be obeyed. Resistance to tyrants is obedience to God. No man's freedom is safe unless all men are free."

Then John Swift, a young lawyer, addressed the applauding assembly. "Burns is in the Court House," he said. "Is there any law to keep him there? It has been said that Americans and sons of Americans are cowards. If we allow Marshal Freeman to carry away that man, then the word cowards should be stamped on our foreheads." The crowd roared. "Tomorrow Burns will have remained [in jail] three days, and I hope tomorrow to witness in his release the resurrection of liberty. This is a contest between slavery and liberty, and for one I am now and forever on the side of liberty!"

The audience shouted, "Yes! Yes! Liberty! We, too!"

Wendell Phillips, lawyer, abolitionist crusader, and orator, rose to speak next. Many said he had the most sparkling blue eyes they'd ever seen. They gleamed brightly at the audience now. Phillips began quietly: "I have been talking seventeen years about slavery . . ."

"Hear! Hear!" hollered someone in the crowd. There were cries of "Shhh! Quiet, there—Wendell Phillips has much to say."

". . . and it seems to me," Phillips continued, "I have talked to little purpose, for within three years two slaves can be carried away from Boston. Nebraska [the Kansas-Nebraska Bill] I call knocking a man down, and this spitting in his face after he is down."

A hush settled over the great hall.

"When I heard of this case and that Burns was locked up in that Court House, my heart sunk within me." Wendell Phillips bowed his head. He next raised it and let his gaze travel around him, fixing on an intense face here and another there.

"See to it, every one of you, as you love the honor of Boston, that you watch this case so closely that you can look into that man's eyes." His deep voice rang out through the hall. "When he [Burns] comes up for trial get a sight at him—and don't lose sight of him."

The audience broke in, "We won't! We won't lose him! Never!"

"If Boston streets are to be so often desecrated by the sight of returning fugitives," Phillips continued, "let us be there, that we may tell our children that we saw it done. Fellow citizens, I will not detain you here any longer."

There were cries of "Go on! Go on!"

"Faneuil Hall is but our way to the Court House where, tomorrow . . ."

Cheers rose and swelled, rolling in waves from the back of the hall forward.

". . . where the children of Adams and [John] Hancock are to prove that they are not bastards. Let us prove that we are worthy of liberty," Wendell Phillips finished.

Feverish shouts of praise rang out, and long applause followed.

Reverend Theodore Parker next stood to speak. Parker was as ungraceful as Phillips was elegant. Often, his admirers watched affectionately as he walked and stumbled, preoccupied, along the city streets. Short of stature, with a massive head of dark hair, he had a dark complexion, and his large, dark eyes stared out with deadly calm behind his spectacles. Occasionally he coughed hard, as though ill with a serious congestion. But now he pursed his lips, then smiled sardonically at the assembly. "Fellow-subjects of Virginia!" he said.

Instantly, there were loud cries of "No! No! You must take that back!"

"Fellow-citizens of Boston, then——"

"Yes! Yes!" the crowd answered.

"I come to condole with you at this second disgrace which is heaped on the city. . . ." Parker thrust his hands into his pockets and looked heavenward. "There was a Boston once. Now there is a North suburb to the city of Alexandria, Virginia—that is what Boston is."

There were hoots and laughter at those words.

"And you and I, fellow subjects of the State of Virginia—"

"No! No!"

"I will take it back when you show me the fact is not so," Parker said, and went on: "I am an old man. I have heard hurrahs and cheers for liberty many times; I have not seen a great many *deeds* done for liberty. I ask you, are we to have *deeds* as well as words?"

The tumultuous crowd answered, "Yes! Yes!"

Reverend Parker then proposed that the meeting be adjourned and that they all gather at Court Square in the morning at nine o'clock. "Those in favor of the motion will raise their hands." There were numbers of hands raised, but a hundred voices yelled, "No, tonight!"

"Let us take him out!"

"Let us go now."

"Come on!"

One man rushed frantically about, crying, "Come on!" but none seemed ready to follow him.

Someone else shouted weakly, "Let's pay a visit to the Revere House—where the slavers stay!"

Reverend Parker then called, "If you propose to go to the Revere House tonight, then show your hands."

Some hands shot up.

"It is not a vote," Reverend Parker said. He realized he was shouting and becoming hoarse. He coughed. His chest ached him now, but he continued.

"We shall meet at *Court Square, at nine o'clock tomorrow morning.*"

The audience shouted cheers and slogans so loudly that few could hear him. A voice rose on the air. "The slave shall not go out, but the men that came here to get him shall not stay in. Let us visit the slavecatchers at the Revere House tonight!"

The crowd gave riotous approval, and those on the platform did not know how to control the excitement. The noise rose to a frantic pitch.

Thomas Higginson and Martin Stowell had planned to give a signal that would turn the crowd toward the Court House at the height of the meeting; the crowd could then free Burns, they hoped. But now it seemed too late. Neither Higginson nor Stowell had dreamed the gathering would be so turbulent. Chances were that a signal would not even be heard by those who were to lead the crowd to Court Square to free Anthony Burns.

Amid the uproar, Wendell Phillips took charge. Standing straight and tall, he uttered only a few words and the seething noise dissolved into complete stillness.

"Let us remember where we are," Phillips said quietly, "and what we are going to do. You have said, tonight, that you are going to vindicate the fair fame of Boston. Let me tell you, you won't do it by groaning at the slavecatchers at the Revere House—by attempting the impossible act of insulting a slavecatcher. If there is any man here who has an arm and a heart ready to sacrifice anything for the freedom of an oppressed man, let him do it tomorrow. If I thought it would be done tonight, I would go first." He struck the air with his fist.

"I don't profess courage," Phillips continued, "but I do profess this: when there is a possibility of saving a slave from the hands of those who are called officers of the law, I am ready to trample any statute. But wait until the daytime. You that are ready to do the real work, be not carried away by indiscretion which may make shipwreck of our hopes. *The zeal that will not keep till tomorrow will never free a slave.*"

The crowd cheered and applauded long and hard at such perfect opinion. Swayed by Phillips's judgment, it began to calm down.

Suddenly, a man at the entrance of the hall frantically waved his arms, trying to get the attention of the stage. He shouted: "Mr. Chairman! Mr. Chairman! I am just informed that a mob of Negroes is in Court Square, attempting to rescue Burns. I move we adjourn to the Court House."

That was the signal Higginson and Stowell had planned—and all had heard! But how were those who had been party to the plan ever to get to the front of the crowd, to lead them? As it was, they were at the back on and around the speaker's platform as the crowd surged away from them.

Faneuil Hall became the scene of wild disorder. The mass of people on the first floor ran head-on into the mass streaming down from the galleries. The hall emptied and the crowd burst forth in waves to overflow in the streets. There axes, axe handles, clubs, and guns were provided by a few of Higginson and Stowell's party in the street. Shouts of "To the Court House! To the rescue, come on!" resounded as the crowd advanced to Court Square. There it broke up into smaller packs. Without leaders to make order of them, they seethed and roiled. And turned into an angry mob.

———

80

The room in which Anthony was confined, high up in the court building, was on the very side where the mob hoped to gain entrance. But Anthony as yet had no inkling it was coming, nor did his captors. In fact, he had been so miserable this evening, thinking on his friends Reverend Grimes and Coffin Pitts, that, close to tears, he had gone deep within himself again, seeking solace. He found it, on the road with Whittom and the other Jims in the time far back in his childhood. Even the bad parts of that trip to the Hiring Ground were of some comfort. At least they belonged just to him, and no one could buy them or sell them away from him.

10

WINTER 1846

ANTHONY was late getting himself and his charges to the Hiring Ground. That was because Simon had a stomach upset. Often, when Simon became fearful of what might happen to him, he would get cramps in his stomach.

"I cain't go no farther widout resting," Simon told Anthony. "I sure cain't."

"We got another hour before we stop," Anthony said, quietly but firmly. They'd been going five hours. Later he would be sorry he'd said that. He knew all of them, Whittom and Efrum and Luther, and himself, too, had been as tired as they could be. But he had not reckoned Simon to be as sick as he was.

Knew he was small, Anthony thought later, but he allus so full of sayings and tells and riddling. . . .

Simon had got cramps that doubled him over. At first the boys thought he was pretending.

"Get on up, yo black thang thar," Efrum said, teasing. "You some white skillet now, come be Missy Pale, gone sleep 'n' snore all the dayclean long."

Simon made a fist and swatted Efrum for calling him Missy and pale. Then he gagged and brought up green bile. They watched him grow sicker under the sun, not knowing what to do.

"Some shade," Anthony said finally. "Let's get 'im under the trees."

"Some water," Luther said. "I'll fetch it." He got fresh water from the stream not a half a mile away. He trotted there and back, never once complaining.

They each tried to do as much as they could for Simon. "I coulda stopped awhile," Anthony muttered. He had his hand across his eyes. "Worrying about ole Mars—who care, him?"

"It all right," Simon said, hardly above a whisper. Though he was feeling sick, he was more frightened of whatever was to come. "Y'all go ahead. I be right chere. You tell Mars come get me. It don't matter none."

He knew they couldn't leave him. To leave a fellow, a slave on the road, meant a certain lashing for all of them, the leader and the followers. Simon would fare worst of all. Nobody cared much about a slave who often was sick. And Simon was born frail—everyone knew that. If Anthony and the others left him, Mars would say he runned away; he had the run-off sickness, and would get whipped too hard, too long. He might even die.

An hour or so later, Simon was rested enough for them to go on. One time Anthony carried him on his back. Then Luther did the same, carrying Simon piggyback awhile.

Luther and Anthony took turns. It was almost fun. Simon

wasn't so very heavy. Whittom and Efrum joined the turn taking, until Simon felt better and said, "I ain't that sick." Then they stopped awhile. They were all tired out; and they were hours late, anyway.

They arrived at the Hiring Ground at dusk. Simon was still feeling poorly, so they helped him along, keeping a watchful eye out for Mars Charles Suttle, too. At length they found him in a tavern with the other masters. Anthony went in alone. The others waited outside by the door.

Anthony dropped to one knee before Mars Charles. He swept the cap off his head and bowed.

"Ah, boy!" Mars Suttle said. "Where you been at all this day? You boys been playin' about, I suspect. I ought to whip you!" This last was said for the benefit of the men with Mars Charles. Owners from the estates near Suttle's, they knew he would not lay a hand on his top boy.

Anthony, still on his knee, shook his head. He did not look up, did not speak, but remained motionless, as he knew this was what Mars Charles wanted. He knew that Mars would be looking around proudly at his friends.

I his most prized, other than his breeders, Anthony thought. Got to be just right, all times, 'cause of bein' the leader of Jims, me, and for Simon's sake. Buckra folks always do like me, 'cause I ain't talk back, I ain't run.

Mars Charles slapped him smartly on his head. Anthony rose and stood at attention before him with his eyes still downcast. He held his cap against his chest, his free hand straight at his sides. His position there before the master was one of a careful, respectful slave, bright but not so much so as to threaten the master's wisdom. A leader boy, one who could control others of his kind, but one who dared never challenge his owner. Both master and slave overplayed this for the benefit of those watching closely.

"Anytime you be wantin' to sell that boy, you lemme know," said an owner. It was Mars Archibald Davenport. Anthony knew the voice. "You got tight discipline there—all yours Jims the same?" he questioned.

"They all right, with my hand over Tony's on 'em," Mars Charles said. "An' I ain' sellin' Tony anytime soon," he added, chuckling. He grabbed Anthony by the neck and held him up in an arm lock. He commenced rubbing Anthony's head with his knuckles so fast and hard that the heat burned Anthony's scalp.

"Huh! How's that, huh? Lemme heah ya holler, boy!" Mars Charles said.

"Ow! Ooow!" Anthony hollered. The owners laughed uproariously. So did Mars Charles, eyeing his friends to gauge the effect. Anthony looked so comical, like a ragamuffin, like something rubbery brown and on a string. He knew how to make himself go limp and take the burning sensation. He knew how helpless and stupid he must look.

The next moment Mars Charles flung him as hard as he could toward the doorway. Anthony slipped and almost fell but quickly righted himself. He hadn't expected to be manhandled just then and had not been ready. Mars Charles yelled at him crossly, "You wait outside for me. And all my Jims better be waitin' with you, too!"

Outside, Anthony trembled with fury in the circle of

his friends. They'd heard Mars hollering. Now they looked away from Anthony as he fought with himself to control his pain and humiliation. They knew it was one thing to be the leader of them, and another to be able to stand the abuse. In a way, Anthony stood in front of them on that score. And he made it easy for them all by shouldering the burden himself.

Simon was seated on the pathway, his back to the wall of the tavern, away from the front. He had his eyes closed. The others were close around him. Whittom had some scraps of food.

"Trying to get him eat somethin', but he won't have it," Whittom said. "Say it's rotten. It look all right to this here hongry boy."

" 'Tis rotten—can smell it," Anthony said quietly, resentment at Mars still in his voice. "Got to get Simon on his feet now," he added. "Mars want us by the door when he come out. Y'all be ready for anythin'. Don't know what's got in him. Most likely, all so many slaves and buckras together. He showing off."

"Lorda mercy," Efrum said. "Do he plan to sell us all?"

"Ain't gone sell us 'less cause it our own selfs," Anthony said. "He gone rent us, hire us out. That's why Simon got to stand up and look strong as he can. Simon? Get up now."

Sweat beaded Simon's forehead as he made the effort to rise. The others helped him.

"Good," Anthony said. "You sweat and you fever fall off, too."

"Oh," Simon murmured. "Oh. Oh."

"You sick agin?" Luther asked anxiously.

They walked back toward the doorway. Laughter floated out. It was getting dark. They were all hungry, beaten by the long march to town.

Eventually, Mars Charles came out. He simply strode away, and they knew to follow at a distance. He had not looked at a one of them.

Anthony led the Jims after their owner.

Mars Charles led them near the Hiring Ground. He spun around once, seeing that they followed. He pointed to the ground. Then he disappeared in the throngs of people.

"Come on," Anthony said softly to his charges. When they reached the approximate spot where Mars Suttle had last stood, Anthony stopped.

"What," Whittom said.

"Just listen," Anthony said. "That's why Mars Charles have me stop right chere where he pointed. You can hear it."

They listened. They could hear a babbling a ways off, like the rise and fall of wind and rain mixed. It made Anthony smile sadly to himself. He breathed deeply and almost cried out. But he held himself in.

"Come on," he said hollowly.

"Is it ev'body?" asked Efrum.

"Sure does sound like it," said Anthony.

It wasn't long before they came upon everybody. The sight of it caused small Simon to catch his breath. It was as if Anthony read his mind. "You stay close to me," he told them, "else somebody be gettin' all mixed up with everybody and I never will find you in time for hirin'."

"Sure is a lot of us," Efrum said. It was true. Hundreds were present at the Hiring Ground. Slave men, women, and children. Black as night, some, and others brown as cinnamon and tan as oak. Lighter, even, light as the first pale hue of dawn. All these were the blacks, everyone. There were women in missy dresses and bonnets, worn for so many weeks that they were filthy and ruined, rotting off them. There were children in sack cloth, without shoes, shivering. There were men in long shirts and nothing more but their broken brogans and hand-me-down planters' hats. There were men in rags and masters' undergarments. A ruffled, filthy shirt here. A torn velvet coat, sleeveless, there. There were groups of twenty and thirty lying in heaps, exhausted and starving from their long journey, for the masters generally provided no food and no shelter.

They, the slaves, gathered as a comfort to one another. For safety, because they knew they were lost and they could find themselves only in the presence of one another. And tomorrow they would be lost and alone again.

They would eat, they would share, they would buy and barter as best they could. They would try to keep warm. Those close to the cook fires that sprang up all around would move back after a while so others could eat or get warmed. When they dozed, they did so with one eye open.

They cried, laughed softly, prayed, sang the sorrow songs. They would eat and sleep right there, together in the open, all the whole crowd of them.

Anthony picked his way through. Efrum, Simon,

Whittom, and Luther followed. They found a tight space where they could stop. They put Simon between Anthony and Whittom. For the first time they truly rested. A black man came with a ratty, holey blanket. "Who wants it?" he said. "Ain't be much."

Simon looked at it longingly. His face shone in the growing light of fires. "He do," Anthony said, pointing to Simon. "How much?"

"Ain't be much," said the man. "That cap on you head. And that cap on he head." He pointed at Luther.

Luther looked down at his hands. Anthony knew he would hate giving up his fine cap. "Be too much," Anthony said quietly, firmly. He dismissed the man by gazing out over the mass of folks.

"Ain't much," said the man. He stood there a long while, but wouldn't give in. "One cap," Anthony said, with calm assurance.

"Two," said the man. He waited.

They were all still. Next to him, Anthony felt Simon control his shivering. Good ole Simon!

Then it was over. The man snatched Anthony's cap and flung the blanket. He walked away. They wrapped the blanket around Simon.

They lay down. No food, not if they wanted something for the morning. They lay close. The Jims slept. Anthony lay there; he too slept finally. Dreamed he saw Jesus. Mamaw was holding the Christ child in her arms, beckoning Anthony to come join them. They were in the great forest. The baby Jesus smiled, climbed down to walk. He led Anthony and Mamaw to free-dom.

11

MAY 26, 1854

"WH-WHAT?" Anthony said. He started up and felt the hard bench under him.

"Where . . . ?" This was no forest. All at once he remembered where he was. He had been lying on his "bed," a Court House bench in the jury room that was his jail. Now he died inside for the thousandth time, so completely had he dreamed a way out. Captured he had been and still was. Prisoner. Slave.

Dreaming won't change it, he thought grimly.

But the guards, what? Guards were running every which way, snatching up their weapons, buckling their belts. Anthony was hearing a deep, loud noise that sounded like it could shake the building down. What was going on?

He went to his window. There he saw a large number of people scurrying around the square.

The banging was coming from below. What? Men were trying to break the door down!

Anthony held on to the bars, watching as best he could, until the guards dragged him back. They pulled him to the floor against the blank wall away from the windows. And there he stayed, listening, wondering what was happening.

Below, the attack on the Court House had begun.

The crowd attacked on the west side of the court building. A dozen men, both black and white, had a long plank to use as a battering ram against the door. Others had axes. Still more had brickbats that they threw up at windows to break them. Glass rattled and fell in all directions. Men ducked their heads out of the way of flying splinters. The sound of the battering ram and the axes falling echoed throughout the adjoining streets and up in the court building. More people came running into the square. The leaders of the attack shouted: "Rescue him! Bring him out! Where is he?"

The Court House bell rang an alarm. The Marshal's guard of 124 had been quickly roused and were at the ready in every hallway and on the stairs. Unknown to the crowd, Marshal Freeman had indeed expected an attack after the Faneuil Hall meeting. He had made sure the Chief of Police had stationed men outside, and he had received a report from them before the crowd reached the Court House.

Now, with Thomas Higginson leading the assault, the west door was broken open. Martin Stowell was by his side with his gun drawn. Before them were guards with guns and cutlasses. There were shouts and startled cries as cutlasses whipped through the air. Higginson felt a swipe of pain against his chin, and then a warm trickling. Shots were fired.

Suddenly, one of the Marshal's guard, a truckman named Batchelder, fell to the floor, bleeding from his stomach. He said he was stabbed. Other guards managed to get the door closed, and braced themselves against it to keep it shut.

The fallen Batchelder was carried into the Marshal's office. He died almost at once of his wound, which had severed an artery in his abdomen.

Meantime, all the attackers were on the outside, including Thomas Higginson, who was bleeding heavily from the chin. He urged his comrades on but they were slow to move forward.

"You cowards!" he exclaimed. "Would you desert us now?"

Almost at once, some of the attackers, nine or ten of them, were taken by the Chief of Police and his men, who had finally reached the front of the crowd. Somehow, Thomas Higginson managed to escape. But Martin Stowell did not. He was arrested with the others and taken for disturbing the peace. This quieted the crowd somewhat, and many began to leave the area.

The Mayor at City Hill was notified of the riot by Chief of Police Taylor. He requested two companies of Artillery, one to be stationed in the Court House and the other in City Hall. These and several officers of the municipal government arrived at the Court House by midnight. Half an hour later Court Square was largely deserted.

12

MAY 27, 1854

THE NEXT day was Saturday, the day Anthony Burns was to appear in court again. Very early in the morning, a crowd once again gathered around the Court House. Composed of those for and against slavery, it was seething with anger and rumor. Marshal Freeman, who had narrowly escaped a bullet as he defended the front stairs, had asked the Mayor for a body of United States troops, which the Mayor ordered out at once. Fifty Marines sped into Boston by steamer and were quartered inside the Court House by morning.

From the Navy Yard in Charlestown came another company of Marines, ordered by the Marshal with District Attorney Hallett's approval. They, too, stayed in the Court House.

Very early, also, the Mayor gave orders for the Independent Corps of Cadets and the Boston Light Infantry to assemble in their armories and then report to City Hall. A detachment of Boston Light Dragoons was in readiness at their armory as well.

Later that morning, James Batchelder's body was taken away by the coroner. The crowd, growing ever larger, watched silently as the coffin was placed in a covered carriage and carried away.

As other carriages passed through the Square, the crowd grew boisterous again. Three or four men causing the most disturbance were arrested on the spot, to rounds of cheers and hisses.

The Mayor came out, stood at the entrance to the Court House, and briefly addressed the crowd. He told them to go home, that sufficient force was present to preserve the peace. All laws were to be maintained, he said.

At these words, applause and boos rang out. He then had a notice posted, which read:

> Because of the excitement that now pervades the city, you are respectfully requested to cooperate with the Municipal Authorities in the maintenance of peace and good order. The laws must be obeyed, let the consequences be what they may.

At five minutes after nine o'clock, Anthony was brought to the Court House by six armed guards and escorted to the United States District Court room.

Seth Thomas and Edward G. Parker appeared as counsel for the claimants, Suttle and Brent, and the United States Government. Richard Dana and Charles M. Ellis were there in defense of the fugitive, Anthony Burns. Spectators, as well as officers of the Marine Corps, filled the courtroom.

The examination began at ten o'clock before Commissioner Loring. Charles Ellis immediately asked for a further delay, for the purpose of preparing the case on the part of the fugitive. It wasn't until yesterday, he said, that he or Mr. Dana had felt at liberty to act for Anthony Burns. And only Mr. Dana had had access to the prisoner.

"It therefore stands as if this person was seized yesterday afternoon," Ellis said, "and brought in here this morning for examination. The man is present in this court as a freeman," he continued, "entitled to all the protection the laws can throw around him."

The law ought not be executed, Ellis said, until a case had been made out as clear as daylight and free from doubt. "Your Honor," he continued earnestly, "do consider that this is the only tribunal between the man and perpetual slavery."

Suttle's attorney Edward Parker objected to a further postponement of the case. "The argument is," he said, "that the proceedings here are to settle the case of the man's freedom or slavery. This is not so. It is only a preliminary hearing, to determine the question of sending the man to a place where the question of his condition will be settled, according to the laws which are presumed to exist there. I therefore see no reason for delay."

Richard Dana spoke next. He calmly reviewed the nature of the record, which was the transcript of the record that Charles Suttle had produced from the Alexandria, Virginia, Circuit Court. The transcript had been put in as proof that Anthony Burns was held to service and labor by Suttle. It further stated that Anthony had escaped from the state of Virginia and still owed service and labor to Charles Suttle, his master; it provided a general description of Anthony.

Dana had had a copy of the transcript only since last evening. "The granting of the certificate," he said now, "which would allow the claimant to remove the prisoner from Massachusetts to the State of Virginia, settles the case of Burns finally. Anthony Burns will never go before another tribunal, but might—and Burns himself fears that he would—be sold to go to New Orleans. The claimant, Mr. Suttle, might send him where he pleases, and Your Honor could not help it.

"If the case goes on now," Dana said, "he, Burns, will say and we, his counsel shall say, that he has had no defense. And it is in view of the tremendous consequences of granting this certificate that we ask for a delay."

"I am advised by the claimant, Charles Suttle," said Edward Parker, "that he is willing to sell the slave here in the city for his fair market value."

On hearing Parker, Reverend Grimes of the freeman's church jerked up straight in his seat, stunned by this sudden good news.

The Commissioner quickly gave his decision. He said he looked upon Burns as one who was still to be regarded as a freeman; he knew of no proof yet submitted that he was to be regarded as anything else. He said he thought the question of delay was a sensible one. "I must look at the rights of the parties and see that justice is done. One or two days' delay is not an unreasonable request, and I therefore grant further delay until Monday morning at eleven o'clock."

With the decision made, the spectators, who had packed the courtroom and had had difficulty keeping still, now quietly left. Anthony was taken back to his jail on the third floor. On each landing of the stairs now, squads of Marines and other United States troops were posted with fixed bayonets; and they were in the rooms of each story as well.

Very large ropes instead of chains were used to keep people out of the passages along the outer walls of the Court House. The barricades were guarded by the Boston police, a fact that incensed a local newspaper: "We should like to know what law of this Commonwealth authorizes or *permits* the Boston police to serve as sentries for the garrison in that fortified slave pen, commonly called 'Boston Court House.' But here is a brave array of troops, marshals, police, and enlisted creatures of various sorts— all on duty to crush out the freedom of a poor fellow whose only crime is a decided repugnance to slavery."

Marshal Freeman had telegraphed President Franklin Pierce informing him of the attack on the Court House the night before and stating that one of his own guards had been killed. He informed the President that he had availed himself of the resources of the United States.

The reply from President Pierce came quickly: "Your conduct is approved. The law must be executed."

* * *

THOUSANDS of people were attracted to the Court House after Commissioner Loring postponed the examination and Anthony was taken back to his jail. They included those who were already there for the abolitionist convention as well as those outsiders who had only just heard of the Burns case. Many had come to protest Anthony's capture. There were arrests for drunkenness and one for a knife attack. A man from Worcester stood upon a flour barrel and spoke loudly about abolitionism and the Kansas-Nebraska Bill before he was arrested for disturbing the peace. Rumors flew. It was reported that 400 "colored persons" from New Bedford had arrived in the city in support of Anthony Burns.

That evening the postmortem examination of Mr. Batchelder was made. Soon after, the word was out that Batchelder's fellow truckmen intended to make a protest demonstration at the homes of Wendell Phillips and Reverend Theodore Parker.

After a number of men were seen approaching Phillips's and Parker's houses, the Mayor posted guards to protect them.

Reverend Grimes had much to do himself that Saturday. Having learned in the courtroom Friday that Anthony might be sold, he at once approached Suttle's counsel and was told, "Colonel Suttle has agreed to sell Burns." The sum of sale was to be twelve hundred dollars. But the condition was that it could be made only *after* Anthony had been surrendered to the Colonel.

"But would not the Colonel consent to close the bargain

before that?" asked Reverend Grimes. He, of course, intended to buy Anthony's freedom.

Edward Parker replied, "I think not."

Grimes then went to talk to Marshal Freeman, who referred him to the Colonel.

Colonel Suttle was polite. He spoke at length on the fact that he "owned Tony." It amazed Reverend Grimes that this slave owner would talk to him so freely, as though he and Anthony Burns were not both blacks. Suttle went on to say that he had always treated Tony kindly and that Tony had a good character. But he would not consider selling his slave *before* the surrender. Next, Suttle left Grimes for a long conversation with his lawyer, Seth Thomas. Thomas then told Reverend Grimes that Suttle had agreed to sell his slave *before* the surrender was made.

Grimes was overjoyed.

"Between this time and ten o'clock tonight," he said, "I'll have the money ready for you; have the emancipation papers ready for me at that hour."

Reverend Grimes had no resources of his own. But as Ben Hallett had observed, he was an able fund-raiser. He spent hours going about the city getting pledges from as many people as he could. Some said they were not ready to contribute to the slave's freedom. Many, however, did pledge, and by seven o'clock in the evening, Grimes had pledges for eight hundred dollars. A broker on State Street advanced the money on this pledge, writing his check for the eight hundred dollars in the Marshal's office.

Grimes again went out and spent the rest of the evening

trying to raise the last four hundred dollars. Finally, a sympathetic gentleman lent him the money so that the transaction could go through.

By half past ten o'clock nothing was left to do but execute the bill of sale. Another half hour was taken up by a private talk between Colonel Suttle and his counsel. Then Grimes went one way and Suttle and his lawyers another, to reconvene at the private office of Commissioner Loring. Arrangements had already been made for Loring to draw up the papers.

When Judge Loring arrived, he proceeded to write the bill in these words:

> Know all men by these present, that I, Charles F. Suttle, of Alexandria in Virginia, in consideration of twelve hundred dollars to me paid, do hereby release and discharge, quitclaim and convey to Anthony Burns his liberty; and I hereby manumit and release him from all claims and service to me forever, hereby giving him his liberty to all intents and effects forever. In testimony whereof I have hereunto set my hand and seal, this twenty-seventh day of May, in the year of our Lord eighteen hundred and fifty-four.

The Commissioner sent for Marshal Freeman. The Marshal refused to come. Reverend Grimes' heart sank; now he was sorry he'd sent a messenger up to Anthony Burns to tell him to be ready in a few minutes, that he was leaving his jail.

Judge Loring gathered his papers. And with everyone

following, he went to the Marshal's office, where they found the Marshal and District Attorney Benjamin Hallett.

Hallett objected to the transaction on the grounds that twelve hundred dollars might be satisfactory for the Colonel but that there were other expenses—troops and guards, for example—that could only be settled by a trial of the fugitive. He said the government wouldn't pay a cent otherwise.

Judge Loring then read a portion of the Fugitive Slave Act, which he said made the government responsible.

"But there is an existing law of Massachusetts," said Hallett, "which prohibits the transaction." He began to recite it: *"Any person who shall sell, or in any manner transfer for any term, the service or labor of any negro, mulatto, or other person of color who shall have been unlawfully seized, taken, shall be punished by imprisonment of not more than ten years."*

Commissioner Loring silenced Hallett. "That law you refer to is a law aimed not against selling a man into freedom," he said, "but against selling him into *slavery*." The bill of sale for Anthony had been for his liberty, not his service or labor as specified by the Massachusetts law.

Ben Hallett smiled. It was not a pleasant smile, thought Reverend Grimes. It fairly put a chill around his shoulders.

"Too late, gentlemen," said Hallett.

The Commissioner chose to ignore him. "Colonel, get this over with," he said. "Sign this bill, please, and accept the payment."

Ben Hallett stood very straight, looking at the clock.

"Gentlemen," he said again. "It is after twelve. See for yourselves, look at the clock. Colonel Suttle's signature will never be legal. Sunday has commenced."

All looked at the clock. The hands showed a quarter past twelve. According to Massachusetts law, no business could be transacted on Sunday. Reverend Grimes closed his eyes and said a prayer for Anthony Burns.

Judge Loring gathered up his papers again and turned to Mr. Grimes. "It can be done at eight o'clock on Monday morning," he said kindly. "Come to my office then, and it can be settled in five minutes."

Mr. Grimes turned away in utter disappointment. Exhausted now, he had worked so hard, and for nothing. And Anthony—poor Anthony Burns! Grimes had a carriage waiting at the door of the Court House to bear Anthony away to freedom. Now he asked the Marshal for permission to see Mr. Burns and relieve him of the suspense of waiting in vain for his friends to come.

The Marshal refused. "I shall tell him myself," he said.

There was nothing for Reverend Grimes to do but dismiss the cab. He did this and then went home, feeling sad and defeated.

13

· MAY 28, 1854·

SUNDAY came all too soon, with still more rumors. It was said that the Federal government had sent telegrams that did not favor Anthony Burns' release. Reverend Grimes, hearing this, was fearful of what would happen next.

"THE MAN IS NOT BOUGHT!" a new handbill circulating on Sunday screamed at the public. "He Is Still In The Slave Pen In The Court House. *Be on your guard against all lies*. Watch The Slave Pen. Let every man attend the trial. Remember Monday morning at 11 o'clock."

Sunday church services had commenced all over Boston. In the immense music hall, Tremont Temple, the Reverend Theodore Parker was about to begin his services. He had no pulpit and no altar, only a desk where he sat and watched as the people filed in.

Today there would be not only the Massachusetts congregation in Tremont Temple to hear him, but Southerners as well. Through a note they had informed him they were present. The Southerners, some friends of the

Colonel's, others from Harvard, had come to hear what he would say against slavery.

Parker grinned. Everyone would go away this day with something new to think about.

When the church was full, he stood and stepped forward to begin the morning service. As he looked around, he noticed that people were standing. Chairs had been placed in the aisles. Hundreds, it seemed, had not been able to get inside. But now there was silence. The great space of the hall with its double tier of galleries might have been empty as he spoke.

"Since last we came together," Parker began, "there has been a man stolen in the city of our fathers. He is now in the great slave-pen in the city of Boston. He is there against the law of the Commonwealth, which, if I am rightly informed, prohibits the use of State buildings as United States jails.

"Why is this? Whose fault is this? The fugitive slave bill Commissioner has just now been sowing the wind, that we may reap the whirlwind.

"Edward Greeley Loring, I charge you with the death of that man who was killed on last Friday night. He dies at your hand. I charge you with filling the Court House with one hundred and eighty-four hired ruffians and alarming not only this city for her liberties that are in peril, but stirring up the whole Commonwealth of Massachusetts with indignation. You have done it all!"

Mouths dropped open and clamped shut again. Then noise rose and exploded.

Parker continued calmly. "I have something from Reverend Grimes and Deacon Pitts, at Anthony Burns's special request. It was given to them by him soon after his arrest and confinement."

The crowd hushed. Parker read the message, which, at about the same time, was being read by other ministers in other Boston churches:

"*To all the Christian Ministers of the Church of Christ in Boston.*

"Brothers: I venture humbly to ask an interest in your prayers and those of your congregations, that I may be restored to the natural and inalienable rights with which I am endowed by the Creator, and especially to the enjoyment of the blessings of liberty, which, it is said, this government was ordained to secure.

"ANTHONY BURNS, Boston Slave Pen, May 24, 1854

"Now," Reverend Parker said quietly, "let us pray."

ALL DAY Sunday Reverend Grimes was most concerned that the plans for early Monday morning would come unraveled. So it was that Sunday evening he felt he had to visit Commissioner Loring at his home.

Loring eased Mr. Grimes's mind by saying that he still felt Colonel Suttle would keep their agreement.

"I do desire to have your assurance," Reverend Grimes told him, unable to shake his sense of foreboding.

"Well then, sir," said the Commissioner, "you have my further word that if Mr. Dana or Mr. Ellis can raise any doubt at all to Burns's identity, then the man shall leave the court a free man."

Reverend Grimes got up to be on his way, and Judge Loring thanked him for stopping by. "We have our appointment for the coming morning, at eight o'clock," Loring said. "We will complete the purchase of Burns at that time."

Feeling a great deal better at the sound of those words, Mr. Grimes said good night and went home.

The next day, Monday, he went early to the Commissioner's office. He waited, but Loring never came. Grimes then set off to find the Colonel. Suttle was not at the Revere House when, hat in hand, Reverend Grimes arrived. Grimes finally found him, along with his lawyers and his agent, William Brent, with Ben Hallett and Marshal Freeman in the Marshal's office.

Always polite, Mr. Grimes begged their pardon for the intrusion and reminded them that they had an appointment together. He said he was ready, and if the others were ready they should complete the transaction.

"No, suh," said the Colonel. "It was not completed Sat'dy night. I therefo' decline to sell my boy. Let the trial go on." He added, courteously enough, "After Tony gets back to Virginia, y'all can have him."

"But, sir, it was not our fault—Saturday night—" Reverend Grimes began.

Ben Hallett cut him off. "When Burns has been tried and carried back, and the law executed, you can buy him," Hallett said. "And then I will pay one hundred dollars toward his purchase."

"But the man is ours," Mr. Grimes pleaded. "They have already said so. There was a verbal agreement."

"The laws of the land cannot be trampled upon," said

Hallett. "A man has been killed, and that blood must be atoned for." He pointed to the spot where James Batchelder had died on the Marshal's office floor.

There was nothing else to say. Reverend Grimes left, amazed and frustrated. It stunned him how events had turned for the worst so suddenly. As he went about town to collect the pledges made by the subscribers to the purchase of Anthony Burns, he found that they, too, had changed their minds.

"If they try him, I refuse to give a cent for his purchase," said one man. He seemed more concerned for Boston than for Anthony. Apparently the gentleman didn't want his fair city to be known as having supported the Fugitive Slave Act. Reverend Grimes discovered that most who had pledged money were of the same opinion.

Meanwhile, for Anthony, Sunday had come and he was still a slave. After Saturday night had worn on and on and still no word had come to him from Reverend Grimes, he had expected bad news. Then the Marshal had come bearing it, to tell him he would not go free, not yet. And his spirit had plunged to the depths of despair. He no longer hoped for anything. Justice, goodness—nothing and no one, even Reverend Grimes, seemed capable of beating the force of the slavery power.

Didn't I run away to here? What more must I do? Anthony wondered. They told me—what did the man Dana say? That even if I runned away, the slavers must *prove* through the law that I had run.

Even if I am Anthony Burns and have said so, *they* must prove that I am me, in the court.

Court. It's coming. Soon now. He bowed his head.

Guards came near, passed him, talked to him, fed him. He ate listlessly. He did not speak when spoken to. All day Sunday they left him alone.

Alone. Anthony was deeply so, far back in his mind where it was ever clear who was the slave and who was not. Ah, boys! he thought vaguely, back in his mind. Them ole times, we was all the little that we had!

14

WINTER 1846–1847

"COACHMAN! COACHMAN! I seek a straight-backed coachman!" The slave owner shouted these words from the raised platform in the open space in front of the town market. This was the Hiring Ground, where Anthony had brought his charges, and it was feverish with busy spectacle and noise. The platform had been built three feet high and square so all could see. Every so often some planter or his assistant would step up onto the platform to begin shouting for the kind of "boy" he wanted. "Coachman!"

The owner now on the platform looked over the youths pushed forward by their masters. He jumped down, stalked about importantly inspecting slaves, and then spied Colonel Suttle, who was standing to one side close to his boys. Casually, the man came up. He stood with his legs wide apart and his hands clasped behind him. He stared down at Whittom and then spoke directly to him, as was the custom.

"Whose boy are you?" he asked.

"Con'l Charles Suttle's, oveh by Stafford County, suh," Whittom said.

"You be the Colonel Suttle, suh?" asked the slaver, turning to Suttle. He was a big man, slim, but with a powerful chest and arms.

"Colonel Charles Suttle, at yo' service," Suttle said, smiling broadly. "All these my boys," he added. He saluted the slave owner.

"I am Ebenezer Caldwell, from near heah, suh." The owner bowed stiffly to Suttle, noting that the Colonel did not seem completely well off. Though he was dressed properly, Suttle's attire appeared to be considerably soiled, and his boys had no new clothes. That would leave the buying of fresh apparel to their new owners or employers. Well, that was all right, Caldwell thought, but the master could have shown a bit more gentlemen's class than he had.

"And him, the big one?" asked Caldwell.

"Name of Whittom, but I calls 'em Jim," Suttle said.

"Calls all mine Amos," Caldwell said. "Well, Jim, what can you do?" he asked Whittom.

"I can do mos' anythin'," Whittom said, as though he didn't care about anything. He didn't fancy the slaver, saw cruelty in his eyes.

Without warning, Charles Suttle slapped Whittom across his face with the flat of his hand. He was furious. For Whittom had meant an insult by not telling in detail what he could do. "Ask you somethin', you bettah say it right!" Suttle told him angrily.

"I 'po'gize, I 'po'gize! I ain't mean nuttin' wrong, boss," Whittom said to the masters.

"Excuse my Jim, suh. I 'pol'gize, myself, to you, suh," Suttle said to the slaver. "Don't know what gets into 'em. They gets here and has to act up first thing!"

Caldwell sighed, nodding. "It's all so many nigras in one place," he said. "They get excited when they smells a great bunch of 'em togethah."

"Ain't it the truth!" Suttle said, and grinned at this fine-looking gentleman.

Again Ebenezer Caldwell studied Whittom, as the Colonel spun him around to give the slaver a good look.

"Stick out your tongue, Jim," Colonel said.

Whittom stuck out his tongue. Caldwell peered down his throat, turning him around to see better. He looked up his nose and in his ears. He lifted his eyelids and studied the whites of Whittom's eyes. He felt his glands, in his throat and his groin. The latter test made Whittom wince with pain.

Lastly, he made Whittom jump up and down with his arms straight at his sides, then over his head. "Now," Caldwell said, slowly and carefully, "what can you do, Jim?"

"I can stoke fire," Whittom said quickly. "I can drive a hoss, both saddle and buggy. I can make bread. I can run errands. I can sweep and warsh walls and mop floors."

"He's a big un, all right," the Colonel said. "He's a mite slow, but he can still do 'bout anything you want."

"Can you run my coach and take care of the horses?" the slaver asked Whittom.

"I can do that!" Whittom said loudly. He had seen the dark look of warning on Colonel's face. He knew the Col-

111

onel was going to get a fair price for his labor. Whittom danced around. "I can do this an' that an' anythin'; I can coach any ole hosses!"

The Colonel and Caldwell laughed. "I like a boy got a humorous streak," Caldwell said.

"Suggest you take on t'other Jim there, the small one, then," Colonel said. He nodded toward Simon. "He one of them liar boys, keep ev'body in a good humor with his tellin's. He and big Jim together make quite a twosome— coach and footman, don't you know!"

Caldwell looked Simon over, walking around him. Anthony, who had been quietly alert and listening, kept his head bowed. He had told the Colonel Simon had been sick. There was no way to avoid it. Simon looked sick to anyone who knew him well. But there was the chance that Caldwell would take the boy for a "high yellow-pillow." That meant he was soft, good for clowning. Pale skin and soft, pale hands. Some masters, cruel like Caldwell, used them as entertainment in the big house. Perhaps Simon would get to tell his "lies" to the mistress and her ladies at the Caldwell plantation. If so, he would not have to work outside in weather under the overseer.

"All right then!" Ebenezer Caldwell said, pinching Simon's cheek hard. "I'll hire me a boy and a 'girl-y' for one year!" He slapped Colonel Suttle on his back as if to strike the bargain.

He and Suttle retired to one side to arrange the business undertaking in writing. The "boys" stood close around Simon.

There were tears in Simon's eyes.

———

112

"Never you mind," Anthony said, only loud enough for his charges to hear. "Maybe I be close by and come visit sometime. Maybe can talk Colonel into lettin' me go see how y'all farin'."

"It be all right," Whittom said to Anthony. "Simon with me—I'll protect him. They ain't goin' get past me!"

But they all knew it was likely that poor Simon would be on his own. There was nothing to be done if Simon stayed sick with stomach pains. For then he would most certainly be sold away. They none of them spoke any more about it. But the air they breathed was grim now.

Every now and again one of them must prance around, making broad statements as to his abilities. He would boast that he could do a hundred different labors. It didn't matter if he could or not. It was only necessary that he sound like he could.

Soon the Colonel was back, and one by one they were hired out. Whittom and Simon went off with their new employer. The last Anthony saw of them, they were sitting under a tree, eating food that Caldwell had provided. Whittom had a new cap, and Simon had one too. They both had on fairly new shoes. They did not look as if they were too badly off as they waited for the new master to finish his hiring of slaves.

As for Anthony, he was obliged to go off next. Colonel Suttle stood by when a gentleman named Mr. Foote was attracted by the serious and generally forthright appearance Anthony made. Anthony for his part didn't like the looks of Foote. But no matter. When Mr. Foote asked the question, "What can you do, boy?" at once Colonel Suttle replied for Anthony, "Suh, my head Jim here can do *any-thin'*."

"Well then," Foote said, "I'm wantin' your Jim to tend the steam engine in my sawmill."

"He can do it!" Suttle said swiftly, before Anthony could tell him he had no idea about sawmills, let alone steam engines. A bargain was quickly made, with seventy-five dollars being the price for Anthony's services for the year. Anthony and Mr. Foote left the Hiring Ground right after the arrangement was fixed.

Mr. Foote lived with his wife at Culpeper, bordering Stafford County. They were Northerners, Yankees, but they might as well have been the lowest of the South's slave masters. It wasn't long before Anthony discovered that Mrs. Foote beat young slaves without mercy. She would strap them to planks on their stomachs, faces downward, on the ground. Anthony watched helplessly one day as Mrs. Foote took up a strip of board cut with holes and roughened with tar and sand. She struck a child's back with the board. Anthony winced as the air drawn through the holes made a high whistle. The child screamed and cried. And by the time Missy Foote had finished the beating, blisters had formed on the child's skin. The sand had made the pain much worse, and the child fainted.

This method of beating was quite common, Anthony had heard, although he'd seen it only a few times. The sand increased the stinging pain but did not deeply cut the flesh to diminish the market value of the slave.

He was never beaten, but he and the other slaves were always hungry. Sometimes the single slice of meat he was given for supper was so thin, he could hold it up and see the sun shine through it. The only good thing that came out of the experience at the Footes' was the fact that there was a daughter who was friendly and secretly helped him along with his reading.

One day, after about three months, Anthony was busy at his duties in the mill. Without warning, Mr. Foote set the machinery in motion. Anthony let out a bloodcurdling cry of pain. His hand was caught in the wheel. When he saw his blood splatter everywhere, he fell unconscious.

Later, when he came to, his hand was broken and swollen beyond recognition. The pain was terrible. A house woman cleaned the dried blood and dirt away and put medicine on it for him. It was only then that Anthony saw how seriously wounded his hand was. The woman bound it tightly, to hold in the swelling, she said. He sucked in his breath and nearly cried; his hand felt as if it would explode.

It was a week before the swelling went down. Then Anthony had the wrappings taken off and replaced with clean ones. He saw the awful disfigurement. His hand no longer seemed to belong to him. Only the pain was his. It never went away, not even when he slept. He was feverish and sick to his stomach most of the time. He could not get the vision of his blood spurting out of his mind. And since he could not work, Mr. Foote decided to send him back to Colonel Suttle.

He went back. The Colonel was there to greet him, looking concerned about him. "Tony, boy," he said, by way of sympathy. "It's a pity, m'boy, a great shame."

Wincing, Anthony held up his broken hand. "That's *anythin'*," he said. For the Colonel had said to Foote when Foote first inquired about him, "He can do *anythin'*."

Anthony continued to suffer with pain. He could not work, and Suttle, feeling guilty, allowed him to go about the place as he pleased. Often he would wander into the forest to pray as Mamaw had taught him. Sometimes he actually saw Jesus standing before him. The Lord's robes were whiter than snow.

"Yea, Lord!" Anthony would murmur to Him. And it would seem that Jesus smiled and spoke to Anthony's mind without moving His mouth. Always, Jesus was kind and gentle.

At other times, Anthony felt the Devil near. And if he dared turn around, he would see the evil serpent of Satan.

"Get away! Get gone from me!" he hollered at it, and worked himself up so that he became feverish again. Crying frantically for Mamaw, he'd run from beneath silent evergreens in terror. He was only just thirteen years old, still a boy and utterly lonely. And it was from these experiences and visitations in the forest that he decided he would serve God and become a slave minister for his people.

AGAIN AND AGAIN Anthony fought his hopelessness by gathering a small congregation of slaves. Occasionally they would meet in the kitchen of a friendly white person. More often they gathered in one of their own rough cabins. Anthony would lead his people in prayer and speak to them of the Gospel and the great King, Jesus.

What he did, preaching, was a violation of Virginia

law, but he fortunately never ended up in the "cage," the temporary outdoor cell for slaves who disobeyed, because Mars Suttle gave Anthony permission to preach. As the slave preacher, he performed marriages among the black subjects and presided over the burial of the dead.

A slave might die during the week, but no funeral could take place that would upset the routine and discipline of the Colonel's Jims and Janetys. The body was placed in a box and put into the ground without delay or ceremony. A few shovels of soil were thrown in, but nobody stopped work to notice. On the following Sunday all the slaves and Charles Suttle would present themselves to the box, and they would cover the grave with earth. They would pray. Anthony would lead the prayers; he would preach until Mars Charles said it was enough, not to take on so. Then the slaves would sing the sorrow songs, the hymns of slavery.

At these times the Colonel smiled on Anthony and the others. He did so love the nigra music. Then it was over. He would leave them to bury the dead in the plain orange box.

In Virginia no monument marked the spot where a dead black was laid to rest at last. Maybe a tree branch carved nicely or a stone marked with a personal sign signifying the man or woman or child in the ground to the other slaves. That would be all that there was to show a life had ended.

"I CAN DO most *anythin'!*" came to his memory. It was a year later. He was back at the Hiring Ground. His hand had been broken and then healed. A man was speaking—

a slave owner from Fredricksburg, Virginia. "Well, I keep a tavern. What does that say to you, Jim?" said the man.

"Says I can sweep up that tavern, suh," Anthony answered. "Say I can warsh them tankards. I can wipe them tables up good, suh!"

"I sholy mean it when I tell you," said Colonel Suttle to the tavern keeper, "my head Jim can do mo' with one hand than a bunch o' them otheh boys can do with two hands apiece."

"I believe it," the tavern man said. "The lame work harder."

"Indeed, they do, sholy," Suttle said.

Anthony made one hundred dollars that year for his owner, Mars Charles Suttle. He had long since left the Footes behind.

And the next year he found a new place to work in the same town. It was a place where medicines were stored and sold—an apothecary shop. Anthony remained true to his purpose of learning ever more reading and writing by often changing his place of labor. For only this would help him to his secret goal—freedom.

One day, when he went into the employer's kitchen to eat, he met there the black woman other slaves called a "two-head"—she was a seer. Everyone knew her as Maude Maw.

After introducing himself, he asked, "You can read all what ain't be yet, for true?"

"Done seen behind me, all-time," Maude Maw said, and paused a moment before she went on, "Now can see before me when it please me."

A two-head for true, Anthony thought. "Yessum, well,

118

will it please you to see before you to where I might stand?" Anthony asked.

She stared at Anthony a long time. In a moment it felt as if heat came to him out of her gaze. He felt slightly dizzy and his eyes began to tear, as though he cried. Yet he felt utter calm inside himself. He was unafraid.

She broke the spell, then, by looking down at the table. After that she avoided looking directly at him.

Anthony breathed deeply and waited. He knew she was reading him, the way two-heads could do it. Read him up and down and front and back. That was their way.

"Two cent," she said, "and I will tell you."

Without a word, he got up to get his money. He brought it back and gave it to her, sitting down at the table again. She kindly served him his supper of pork stew and rice. She did not move again until he had finished. Then she cleared the dishes away and wiped the table clean. When all was in order, she sat down across from him. "Hard times," she said in a low voice.

That made him smile. Was there a slave who hadn't had hard times? "Front or back?" he said softly, meaning hard times now, or in the future?

He thought her eyes would swallow him. He would remember them long after he forgot the exact words she had said.

"Wings over Jordan," she said. "Never fear. Wings over Jordan."

"What?"

"Wings over Jordan." She said the words one last time. And then she closed her eyes, ending the conversation.

Later that evening, after he had rested awhile on his

straw pallet of a bed, Maude Maw's hidden message came to him clearly.

"Means I am to get away!" he said out loud. Anthony clamped his mouth shut and looked around him. Nobody had heard, he was sure. But he must be careful.

Means by wings, the bird that flies. And I will be him, bird! he thought.

By the Jordan, Maude Maw meant the river Jordan of Palestine in that holy place of Jesus. It was talked about in the Bible.

Wings over Jordan! If he had once doubted he would be free one day, he did not now. Soon he would spread his wings. Yea mercy, Maude Maw has seen it!

After that, Anthony made better progress. By the time he turned eighteen he felt strong and more confident. He refused arrangements for employment when he suspected the owner wouldn't give him enough time on his own. He worked for William Brent, who was now the Colonel's agent, and then for Brent's brother-in-law. He advanced with his education by mastering the spelling book. And he began to understand the New Testament. Painstakingly, Anthony learned more about the process of writing from the letters of his employers, which he looked into at every opportunity.

He next worked in Richmond, Virginia. At the end of his first year there he changed his employer for the last time. This employer was a druggist named Millspaugh. Because Millspaugh didn't have enough work to keep Anthony busy, he allowed Anthony to find employment on his own. It was a secret between the two of them. "You pay me the sum of one hundred and twenty-five for the year," he said. "I pay it to the Colonel. You pay me a bonus and set the amount. It's a violation of the law, so don't you tell a soul."

So the arrangement was set. Anthony made payment to Millspaugh every two weeks. He was on his own for long periods when no one—not Millspaugh, nor Brent, nor the Colonel—knew his whereabouts. There was time for him to go down to the docks to talk with sailors. These were men who had been free from the moment they were born. They were kind to him, speaking to him man to man and not master to slave.

"You ought to run, Anthony," they did not hesitate to urge him. "What's the worry? We'll help you out."

Wings over Jordan! thought Anthony. Soon he would spread his wings.

15

MAY 29, 1854

A PALE LIGHT gathered around Anthony, enough to make him stir. Awake again, he knew the time was now, and awful. Court House jail.

I'm tired, me, he thought, seeing the light at his prison window. Not future yet. Just another day. Which? Monday? So soon! They say the courtroom business will begin again this day. And still I am a slave.

He heard men stirring. Guards mustering. The whole Court House, it sounded like, was up and ready.

Lord, I flew all this long way to here. Wings. What good did it do? And now they say Mars Charles must prove who I am.

Outside, the Court Square was loud with resentment and rancor. There was a sense of grave danger in the air. Since dawn, thousands of Bostonians and citizens from neighboring towns had gathered, taking note of each movement of troops. At every window were Massachusetts and United States soldiers with their guns at the ready. They gave the massive Court House the look of a besieged medieval keep.

Entrances to the Court House were closed tight, except for one that was guarded by the city police. Reporters could enter here, and those favored among the upper class who had obtained permits from U.S. Marshal Freeman or District Attorney Ben Hallett. All else except officials of the court were barred.

Never before in Boston's history had a court house been closed to the public. The reason was clear: City authorities feared that citizens would rise up in defense of Anthony Burns.

By the time the court opened, Anthony was ready. He had eaten little but he was dressed decently. He had been brought down a back staircase in wrist irons, shielded from the reporters waiting to get into the room, and led into the courtroom.

The Commissioner, Judge Edward Loring, sat upon the bench. He looked weighed down by troubles and the task ahead of him. On Loring's right stood U.S. Marshal Watson Freeman. He was in rather calm good humor this morning.

District Attorney Ben F. Hallett sat at the clerk's desk. Also in their seats and waiting were Charles Suttle, William Brent, a group of Southern friends who had come up from Virginia, and Suttle's lawyers, Seth J. Thomas and Edward G. Parker.

Not far from them and within the bar were Anthony's lawyers, Charles M. Ellis, Richard Henry Dana, and their aide, Mr. Robert Morriss. Flanking them were Theodore Parker, Wendell Phillips, and Reverend Grimes. Several reporters sat nearby. Other privileged and interested spectators were scattered throughout the courtroom.

Anthony sat in the front seat facing the Commissioner, between two grim guards. In front of him, within the bar, stood five more guards with pistols.

The proceedings began with a protest against continuing the case. "I protest not on personal grounds," said Charles Ellis, the junior counsel for Anthony, "but because it is not right and fit. It is not fit that we would proceed while the prisoner sits with shackles on his limbs. It is not fit that we should proceed while the courtroom is packed with armed men, and all the avenues to it are filled with military, making it difficult for the friends of the prisoner to obtain access to him. I protest against proceeding under these circumstances."

"The examination must proceed," replied Judge Loring. "I will give this matter consideration if necessary, hereafter."

Ben Hallett rose and began arguing with the Commissioner in reply to what had been said by Charles Ellis.

"I've already decided that we must continue," said Loring, "and any further remarks are unnecessary."

But Ben Hallett would not be silenced. "The conduct of the Marshal has been called into question," he said. "And I am present at his request to act as his counsel."

"Mr. Hallett," Judge Loring said, "these remarks are irrelevant and entirely out of order."

"These proceedings are necessary because of the conduct of men who got up and inflamed the meeting at Faneuil Hall," Ben Hallett said, "some of whom I see here within the bar, and who are claimed by Mr. Ellis as his friends."

"Mr. Hallett!" Judge Loring cried.

Hallett sneered scornfully at him and would not stop:

"The men who committed murder that night came directly from the incitements to riot and bloodshed which had maddened them in Faneuil Hall. The President of the United States has approved of this course, and the efficient aid which the Marshal has ordered to prevent further violence and murder."

Helplessly, Judge Loring sank back in his seat. The spectators gasped at Hallett's shocking insolence. It seemed that the court had little power over him: Although Hallett should have been cited at once for contempt and ordered into custody, Edward Loring did nothing—but look ashamed. Richard Dana, watching in dismay, guessed that Loring feared Hallett, who gave the strong impression that he represented the Federal government and thus the President of the United States.

Charles Ellis started to comment on Hallett's language when the Judge waved him quiet. Loring said that the examination must proceed. Ellis then asked, in the absence of any record, whether the Commissioner had legal authority in this case. According to Massachusetts statute, a probate judge such as Loring was forbidden to act in slave cases. Loring replied that he was quite qualified and that the case would continue right now. Because his appointment as Commissioner was a Federal one based on Federal authority, he felt this superseded state restrictions.

Now Richard Dana rose.

The case for Charles Suttle had been presented on Thursday, the 25th of May, when Anthony Burns as yet had no one to defend him. Dana demanded the whole examination restart; Loring agreed, ordering the case to commence as though it had not been postponed on Saturday.

The complaint against Anthony was again read by Edward G. Parker, Suttle's junior counsel. Then William Brent was called to the stand to testify as to who he was and who Colonel Suttle was. He said he had acted as Suttle's slave agent in hiring out Anthony to a man named Millspaugh. He finished by saying that the last he'd seen of Anthony was on the 20th day of March, 1854; by the 24th, Anthony was missing. On the following Tuesday, March 28, Brent had informed the Colonel of Anthony's disappearance. But, Brent said, he knew nothing of how Anthony had left Virginia.

After his arrest on May 24th, Anthony had said certain things that could be used against him; he had greeted Charles Suttle as "Master," for one. Now Suttle's lawyers tried to put in these admissions as evidence.

"We object," said Charles Ellis. "The Sixth Section of the Fugitive Slave Act provides that the testimony of the alleged fugitive shall not be taken."

"The admissions and confessions of Burns are a very different thing from testimony," replied Suttle's senior counsel, Seth Thomas.

"It is the height of cruelty to the prisoner," Richard Dana countered, "to take advantage of the only power Burns has under this law—that of speech—while the other party in the suit has his own right and, by these alleged confessions, a portion of the prisoner's."

Even at this early stage of the examination and before Dana had revealed the nature of his defense of Burns, Anthony's fate could well depend on the question of his alleged confessions. It would be up to the Commissioner to decide whether what Anthony said when Suttle confronted him the night of May 24th constituted testimony. For if it did, under Section Six of the Fugitive Slave Act it could not be admitted as evidence and used against Anthony.

Dana distrusted Loring. He worried that the Commissioner would decide against Anthony. During a short recess that was called, his worries deepened, for on making his way back to court, he was stopped by guards brandishing their bayonets and kept waiting at the foot of a staircase until Marshal Freeman decided he could pass.

"This is outrageous!" Dana told Loring once he was back in court. "You need to instruct the Marshal in his proper duties."

"I have no authority to direct the actions of the Marshal," said Loring. All the while, Marshal Freeman stood by, grinning insolently at Richard Dana.

Dana thought Loring *could* exert control over the Marshal if he chose to. But Loring did nothing. So Freeman was showing that he could surround the courtroom, admit or bar individuals from the court at his own whim, and insult the defense lawyers as he pleased—and there was no one to call him to account or to stop him. Worse, behind Marshal Freeman was District Attorney Benjamin Hallett. And behind Hallett stood the power of the President of the United States.

All stacked neatly against the slave, thought Richard Dana.

Under these conditions, the examination continued after the recess. All eyes were riveted on the unfolding drama.

A breathless silence hung in the courtroom above the bowed head of Anthony Burns.

"I am unwilling to prejudice the liberty of the prisoner," said Edward Loring. "But I think that 'testimony' in the law refers to evidence given by a witness and not to confessions or admissions such as Burns may have made."

Dana groaned inwardly.

"Yet the prisoner's counsel may have the right to pass that question for the present," Loring said, "to come back to it later."

In no trial or hearing under this act shall the testimony of such alleged fugitive be admitted in evidence . . . Dana quoted in his head from Section Six of the Fugitive Slave Act.

"We desire that the question as to Burns's admissions on May 24 might be asked," said Seth Thomas, "and that the answers be taken down for future use, if necessary."

Dana held his breath.

Loring agreed and admitted *de bene esse*—"of validity for the time being," which meant the admissions would be taken for the time being, subject to objection or nullification at a later date.

Loring has gone completely against us on this point, Dana thought.

William Brent then related the conversations that took place between Anthony and Suttle the night Anthony was captured. "Burns said he didn't mean to run away, but being at work on board a vessel," said Brent, "and getting tired, he fell asleep. The vessel then sailed with him on board."

128

Their own witness is saying, Dana thought, that Burns did not escape. He fell asleep. . . .

Brent continued: "The first word from Burns when Mr. Suttle went to him after his arrest on Wednesday, the twenty-fourth of May, was 'How do you do, Master Charles?' The next exchange was 'Did I ever whip you, Tony?' The answer was 'No.' The next was 'Did I ever hire you out to where you didn't want to go?' And Burns replied, 'No.' Mr. Suttle's question then was 'Did you ever ask me for money when it was not given you?' The answer was 'No.' Finally, Mr. Suttle asked, 'When you were sick, did I not take my bed from my own house for you?' and the answer was 'Yes.'

"The slave recognized me, then," Brent said. " 'How do you do, Master William?' he said. And then when asked, he said he was quite willing to go back home to Virginia."

That is not at all what Anthony told *us*, Richard Dana was thinking as he began his cross-examination of Brent. He objected to Brent calling Anthony "slave" and said so. He won that point when the Commissioner said, "The witness must not state any person to be a slave without corroborative legal evidence." But no matter how Dana tried in his cross-examination, he failed to get any further evidence that would materially affect the case.

As for Anthony, from the moment Mars Brent had said that he had gone off on the vessel, his mind had taken a leap backward. Sitting in the courtroom, almost in a trance, he thought, I love a woman. And he was back in Richmond, the great port where the tall ships came in on the tide.

16

WINTER 1854

HE HAD met the woman on his rounds for the druggist, Millspaugh, delivering medicines to the back doors and kitchens of the city. She too was a slave.

I must leave her, Anthony realized, after setting his new arrangement for work and payment with Millspaugh. I cannot help it. I cannot stay in Richmond any longer. How would I take her away with me? Best not even to say, "Fare thee well, my love." Oh, mercy! I will give her up. I must. But I swear, I will never have any other, for as long as I shall live.

Anthony roomed in Mr. Millspaugh's own house above the man's bedroom. One night, in the early part of February 1854, he put on four outfits of clothing, with the worn, coarse work clothes he dressed in each day as the topmost layer. Next, he wrapped food and some belongings in a small bundle, which he meant to carry with him. Then he lay down to sleep. There was another slave who shared the room with him, a young clerk. Luckily, he never awoke the whole night. For this was the night that Anthony would run.

An hour before dawn, Anthony left the house and made his way over to the docks. Arriving unseen, he boarded an old Baltimore clipper.

Anthony had a sailor friend on board the ship. At their last meeting they had talked about keeping secrets. "Now you musn't call me by my real name again, Anthony," his friend told him. "Forget you ever knew it. And after this trip, I will forget I ever knew your name."

So Anthony made up a new name. He called his friend Cal Cross. Cal was Calvary, the hill where Jesus died upon the cross.

Cal quickly stowed him away in a place he had prepared. Anthony never knew where it was on the ship, they had gone so stealthily and made so many twists and turns up and down corridors. It was a damp, dark place, no better than a hole and just barely big enough for Anthony, smelling of oil and slime. He could hear the sea slapping against the hull outside. *Let there be no rats in this place!* he asked Jesus.

Hours and hours later, the ship had not moved. Lord! When will she sail? thought Anthony. His hiding place was so small, he couldn't stretch out. It grew hot and uncomfortable, and at last he fell into an exhausted sleep.

Some time later Anthony awoke with a start, barely able to move in his cramped position. The ship, now under full sail, pitched and tossed in the rough water and heavy, contrary winds. Lying on one side with no room to turn, Anthony became seasick. By the time Cal came to see him, Anthony was miserable.

"At the next port," he begged, "put me off, please. I cannot stand it any longer. Put me off the ship!"

"And what becomes of freedom?" asked Cal.

"It dies, because surely I am dying!" Anthony said.

"You are sick, but you will not die," Cal told him. "Here is some fresh water. And I have bread for you—make it last. I'll try for meat tomorrow." Cal left him to his misery.

Two days later the ship docked in Norfolk, Virginia, where it stayed half a day. Then it continued on toward its destination, Boston. Though the passage was to take ten days to two weeks, it took nearly three. Anthony was sick almost the whole time. He was unaccustomed to the February cold and commenced to shiver and shake violently. Not once could he leave his hiding place or change his position from his side. Never was he able to moan or cry out in his pain. Bread and water were what he lived on; he received the nourishment every three or four days when Cal was able to give it to him. At no time was anyone else, the captain or any officer, aware that he was there in hiding.

The ship was headed north. Anthony had never experienced February cold. And before the end of the voyage, his feet were frozen in his boots.

Finally, sometime near the final days of February or the first of March, the ship made the wharf at Boston harbor. After giving Cal a grateful, if hurried, good-bye, Anthony managed to get to shore unnoticed. The morning was gray. Not many people were about. He took on the appearance of an ordinary seaman—who limped. So stiff was he. He found his way to a boardinghouse, where he was able to find a room. After a week he was pretty much recovered from bruises, cold, sickness, and hunger. He could toss and turn on his bed as often as he pleased. And he took particular pleasure in sleeping on the opposite side from the one he'd had to keep to on the ship.

He found work, and it was good work. He became a cook on a flat-bottomed square-end boat called a mud scow. He did well with his new duties, except for one important chore. He was to bake the bread. But no matter how hard he tried, he could not make it rise. And after a week Anthony was let go.

His next employment was with the Mattapan Works in South Boston.

17

MAY 29, 1854

As he sat in the courtroom, Anthony's mind raced. *That letter I wrote to my pastor,* he thought. *I mailed it to brother mine in Richmond, had it postmarked in Canada. But I must have dated it Boston. I do remember, I did that. Never knew how much a little letter could mean. An awful bad mistake. Now, here I be.*

Courtroom voices rushed in, startling him, and he was back from his journey into memory. He bowed down his head and closed his eyes, as if to blot out the sounds. But he could not. It seemed that all of his past had caught up to him in the present.

Seth Thomas for the Colonel was speaking: ". . . to put in the record of the court of Virginia as evidence, that Charles F. Suttle did appear in Alexandria Circuit Court, May 16, 1854, and made satisfactory proof that Anthony Burns was held to service and labor by him. And service and labor are due him from the said Anthony."

Thomas's voice droned on, but what he said held Richard

Dana's rapt attention: ". . . and that the said Anthony has escaped from the State aforesaid . . ."

But by Brent's own testimony, Dana thought, Anthony fell asleep. There was no *escape*!

". . . and that the said service and labor are due him, Suttle, the master of Anthony; and having further proved that Anthony is a man of dark complexion, about six feet high, with a scar on one of his cheeks, and also, a scar on the back of his right hand, and about twenty-three or four years of age, we ask that it be therefore ordered," Thomas continued, "in accordance with an act of Congress—the Fugitive Slave Act respecting fugitives from justice and persons escaping from their masters—that the matter set forth be entered on the record of this Court."

"It is in that case subject to objection from the prisoner's counsel," said Commissioner Loring.

Richard Dana examined the transcript of the record of the Alexandria court. It was certified by the Circuit Court clerk as a true transcript from the court records. "We should have several objections to present against it," Dana said.

Edward Parker for the Colonel said, "The record is decisive of two points: first, that Burns owed service and labor, second, that he escaped."

Dana had to smile. They are contradicting themselves, he thought.

Parker then requested that Loring examine the marks on the prisoner.

"I perceive the scars on the cheek and hand, and take

cognizance with my eye of the prisoner's height," said Loring.

Next, Thomas presented a volume of Virginia laws as evidence. Richard Dana at once objected. "A *book* is here presented to show that a person owes service and labor in Virginia! We deny the sufficiency of the evidence."

"The proper way to prove the law of another state is by books," said Seth Thomas. "If the book is not sufficient, I wish to prove the fact in another way."

"Let the book go in as testimony for what it is worth," Commissioner Loring said.

The evidence on behalf of Charles Suttle now ended. Suttle was pleased that Commissioner Loring had allowed his entire case to be entered, even though Mr. Dana had objected. The court had now been in session five hours, and Suttle's counsel asked for an adjournment. Loring allowed for a half hour's recess to give Dana and Ellis time to make necessary preparations for Anthony's defense.

Richard Dana knew this wasn't enough time to make use of the law library. Why must he handicap me? he thought. Loring was deciding against every objection he or Ellis made. And the Marshal's guard and the military made it impossible for them to come and go freely. Dana felt it was crucial that he get to the law library to study complex questions of the law.

When the court reassembled at three thirty that afternoon, Mr. Ellis opened for the defense, and he was furious. He stated that the time that he and Mr. Dana had had to prepare their case was no more than a day. "This case involves novel questions of law," Ellis said, "but the library has been locked up. The military makes it next to impossible, even for counsel, to enter the courtroom. I am stopped from climbing the stairway by soldiers with their bayonets at my breast. Still, Your Honor, we must go on.

"We shall offer evidence to contradict that produced by the claimant, evidence upon the *facts* at issue. But before stating it, we claim that there is no evidence offered by the claimant that will justify the signing of a warrant of slavery.

"We stand on the presumption of which Your Honor did well to remind counsel, the presumption of freedom and innocence.

"Sir, you sit here, judge and jury," Ellis continued. "You sit to render a judgment which, if against him, no tribunal can review and no court reverse. He, Burns, may be dragged before you without any warrant; you must proceed without any delay; without any charge, on proofs defined only as such as may satisfy your mind, you may adjudge, and your judgment to surrender will be final forever.

"Seized on a false charge, without counsel, the prisoner is to be doomed.

"If such a case stood alone, we feel that it ought to be dismissed. But the prisoner *has a case*." Charles Ellis looked around the room slowly, measuring the effect of his words. The spectators hung on each one. "The complaint alleges," he said carefully, "the only record offered proves, the only witness called testifies to, an escape from Richmond on the *twenty-fourth day of March last*. The witness, Brent, swears clearly and positively that he saw this prisoner in Richmond on the *twentieth day of March*.

"We shall call a number of witnesses to show that the prisoner was in Boston on the *first of March last*, and has been here ever since up to the time of this seizure. This is our defense."

There were stunned murmurings in the courtroom. Commissioner Loring banged his gavel, and the room quieted.

A black freeman, William Jones, was called by Ellis to the stand. Jones testified that he first saw Anthony Burns in Boston on March 1, 1854, and that on the 4th of March he employed Anthony to labor in the Mattapan Works at South Boston. "He worked with me cleaning windows," Jones said. "I agreed to give him eight cents a window; and when he was through, I gave him a dollar and a half." He was able to be certain of the dates, he said, because of notations in a memorandum book that was kept by his employer, a Mr. Russell.

Seth Thomas cross-examined William Jones sharply but got nowhere in shaking his testimony. Finally, the witness was allowed to step down from the stand.

That ended Monday's testimony. On Tuesday, May 30, evidence for the defense continued all morning and afternoon. George H. Drew, the white bookkeeper at the Mattapan Works, confirmed Mr. Jones's statements of the day before. Jones was employed on the first of the month. At that time Drew saw Anthony Burns with him. Drew had no doubt of the identity of the man in the prisoner's box.

Next to take the stand was James F. Whittemore, a member of the Boston City Council and a director of the Mattapan Works. He said he had seen Burns cleaning windows with Mr. Jones on the 8th or 9th of March. He told Dana, "I am a Lieutenant of the Pulaski Guards. I've no particular interest in this case. I am in no way a Free-Soiler or abolitionist."

John Favor was then sworn in. "I am a carpenter," he said. "I saw Jones in my shop in March. He had a colored man with him. He came to get employment for the colored man. When I came to court, I recognized Burns there as the man with Jones. They came to my place about the first of March."

Next was Horace W. Brown. "I am a police officer," he said. "I have seen the man in the prisoner's box before. He was cleaning windows at the Mattapan Works, South Boston. I had worked there as a carpenter before I was a policeman. And I saw Burns at work there a week to ten days before I left there on the twentieth of March. I have not the slightest doubt about this."

With Horace Brown's testimony, the case for the defense ended.

Colonel Suttle and his lawyers and loyal followers had been contemptuous of the first witness, Jones. They had regarded his testimony as a complete lie from beginning to end. But when the next witness, in their eyes a decent white man, took the stand, they turned to one another with some alarm. Their alarm grew when an officer in the Pulaski Guard (which guarded the very Court House now under siege) said he was no abolitionist, but swore he had seen Burns early in March, thus confirming the earlier testimony. Now Colonel Suttle and his group looked very upset.

A total of nine witnesses were called by the defense. Each of their testimonies contradicted William Brent's—that he had last seen Anthony Burns in Virginia on the twentieth of March.

At this point Seth Thomas tried to introduce rebutting evidence. He called Ben True, one of Anthony's guards, who would testify to certain statements that Anthony had made.

Richard Dana objected on the grounds that Anthony's admissions were made under guard and threat, and that they did not form a rebuttal.

The Commissioner ruled that the witness's testimony should be admitted.

Again he was ruling against the defense and Dana.

Ben True stated that Burns had said he had been in Boston about two months and that previously he had been in Richmond, Virginia.

The testimony on both sides was then closed for the day, and the court was adjourned until nine o'clock Wednesday morning.

In the late afternoon after the adjournment there was much excitement in and around the Court House. People were heard to say that Burns would go free, since the evidence so far was proof for the defense. The Southern slave owner could not possibly win, and another fugitive would not be stolen out of Boston.

18

MAY 31, 1854

On Wednesday, May 31, Seth Thomas called several witnesses to rebut and disprove the defense's testimony. A Mr. Cyrus Gould was sworn in. He stated, "Mr. Jones worked for me on the sixteenth and seventeenth of March. I was employed at the City Hall all the month of March. Jones worked there on the tenth two or three hours. I did not see Burns with Jones there at any time. There was no man working with him; two women were working with him."

More rebutting evidence was given, all of it reinforcing William Brent's testimony that Anthony had been in Virginia on the twentieth of March.

Dana then objected that the admissions of a man under arrest should be received at all. He objected that it was not rebutting testimony, that the evidence that Burns was in Boston on the 1st of March was contradictory to the testimony for the claimant that Burns was in Virginia on the twentieth of March. He said, "They, for the claimant, are now simply reinforcing their former testimony."

Seth Thomas argued that this evidence, and Brent's

testimony, proved the identity of Anthony Burns, rather than establishing his whereabouts. "The defense proposes to prove an *alibi*," Thomas said, the alibi being that the prisoner was seen in Boston when the claimant, Suttle, said he was in Virginia. "We introduce our evidence to control their evidence in support of the *alibi*."

Dana renewed his objection.

Commissioner Loring ruled that the rebutting testimony was indeed opposing evidence and admissible. "But I give counsel notice that if I change my mind before the arguments, I will inform you."

Richard Dana had been working up his final argument for the defense. He had written on backs of envelopes and scraps of paper. He felt angry and tired but not at all defeated by the course of the examination. He certainly hoped that Loring would change his opinion as to the admissions Burns had allegedly made. He also knew that in order for Suttle to be entitled to his certificate to return Anthony to slavery, the United States Constitution *and* the Fugitive Slave Act required proof of an *escape*.

Section Ten of the Fugitive Slave Act stated that a record had to show evidence of an escape and evidence that the person escaping owed service and labor to the party of the record—in this case, Charles Suttle.

But the evidence against Burns not only failed to show an escape, it in fact showed the opposite, that *there was no escape*.

Furthermore, the claimant was trying to prove the defendant's identity by using his words against him, when Section Six of the Fugitive Slave Act clearly stated that the testimony of the person claimed could not be taken. William Brent's testimony might identify the alleged fugitive, Burns, but it also proved that Burns did not escape: According to Brent, Anthony Burns said he fell asleep and the boat sailed away with him. There was no *escape*.

And there was another point to be made: Section Six and Section Ten provided for separate and distinct proceedings.

Dana gathered his notes. He would speak from them today.

Ben Hallett had not been in court on Tuesday and had missed the parade of witnesses for the defense. When he heard how badly this "open-and-shut slave case" had turned, he was furious. He stormed over to the telegraph office hoping for some word from Washington, anything that would give him a good reason to keep the large force of United States military in place. Hallett knew that Major General B. F. Edmands, commander of all the battalions and regiments in Boston, was aware of this new turn of events in the Burns case. Edmands wanted to dismiss some of the more than one thousand troops in the city, now that everyone seemed to agree that the fugitive might not be one at all.

But before General Edmands could finish all the paperwork needed to dismiss the troops, Ben Hallett had his message by telegraph from Washington, It was addressed directly to him and it read:

INCUR ANY EXPENSE DEEMED NECESSARY BY THE MARSHAL OR YOURSELF FOR CITY MILITARY OR OTHERWISE, TO IN-

ON WEDNESDAY morning the Adjutant General of the
Army, Colonel Cooper, arrived with Ben Hallett in the
Mayor's office. Colonel Cooper was under personal orders
from President Pierce to bring in two more companies of
soldiers. As a result of this visit, the Mayor that same
morning ordered the state militia to take up positions on
Boston Common on Friday, June 2nd, the day Commissioner Loring would deliver his decision in the Burns case.

While this order was being signed by the Mayor, Richard Dana began to make his final plea for Anthony Burns.

The courtroom was quiet. The silence of the spectators
showed their respect for the authority of Richard Dana.

Only Anthony did not know how renowned was his lawyer. But he was quite aware that what happened now would
seal his fate.

Richard Dana stood before the court as a distinguished
and powerful defender of the oppressed. He was the son
of a poet and the grandson of a Chief Justice of Massachusetts. He believed in the Constitution, which states
under Article IV of the Bill of Rights that people are
protected against unreasonable seizures. Article V states
that no one shall be deprived of liberty without due process of the law. Dana believed in Massachusetts law too,
and knew it to be on the side of right and freedom for the
enslaved. His opening was a stinging rebuke to the Commissioner and others in authority. "I congratulate you,
sir, that your labors, so anxious and painful, are drawing

144

to a close," he said to Edward Loring. "I congratulate the Commonwealth of Massachusetts that she is to be relieved from that dark demon which has rested on her for so many days and nights, making her to dream strange dreams and see strange visions.

"I congratulate her that in due time by leave of the Marshal of the United States and the District Attorney of the United States, her courts may be reopened, and her judges and witnesses may pass and repass without being obliged to satisfy hirelings of the United States Marshal and other bayonetted men.

"I congratulate, too, the Government of the United States, that its legal representative, Mr. Hallett, can return to his duties and that his presence will no longer be needed here in a private civil suit for the purpose of intimidation of this tribunal." Dana's voice shook with emotion, then steadied and calmed.

"I congratulate the Marshal of the United States that the ordinary respectability of his character is no longer to be in danger from the character of the associates he is obliged to call about him.

"I congratulate the officers of the Army and Navy that now they can draw off their noncommissioned men, both drunk and sober, from this fortified slave pen back to their forts and fleets, which have been left in peril so that this great Republic might add the trophy of one more captured slave."

Dana paused, looked long at Anthony with utter sympathy, and turned back to the Commissioner. Speaking softly, he said, "I offer these congratulations in the belief that the decision of Your Honor will restore to freedom this man, the prisoner at the bar, whom fraud and violence found a week ago a free man on the soil of Massachusetts. We have a right to expect from Your Honor a strict adherence to the rule that this man is free until he is proved a slave beyond every reasonable doubt.

"We have before us a free man. Colonel Suttle says there was a man in Virginia named Anthony Burns; that this man is a slave by the law of Virginia; that he is *his* slave, owing service and labor to *him*; that he escaped from Virginia into this State, and that the prisoner at the bar is that Anthony Burns. He says all this. Let him prove it *all!* Let him fail in one point, let him fall short the width of a spider's thread, in the proof of all his horrid category, and the man goes free.

"The man they seek has never lived under Colonel Suttle's roof since he was a boy. He has always been leased out. He was under lease to a Mr. Millspaugh when he disappeared. As Colonel Suttle could not authorize Burns to leave Virginia, so neither could he forbid his leaving it. He has simply nothing to say about it. One part of the testimony showed that Burns, at the time of his alleged escape, owed service not to Suttle, but to Millspaugh. This was in flat contradiction to the record. What right then has Suttle to claim Burns? Until the lease expired, Millspaugh had the sole right of possession and control.

"The claimant's witness, Mr. Brent, puts his case resolutely, that the man he means was in Richmond up to the twentieth of March. We have proved that the prisoner was here on the first and fifth and tenth and eighteenth. The claimant must show that the prisoner owes service

146

and labor to Colonel Suttle, by the laws of Virginia, and that he escaped from that state into Massachusetts.

"Perhaps the claimant will say," Dana continued, "that the record is final as to the facts of slavery and escape, and that the only point open is that of identity. That is so if he adopts the proper mode of proceeding to make it so. Section Ten of the Fugitive Slave Law provides that the questions of slavery and escape shall be tried in the state from which the man escaped and the record of this would be final.

"Section Six of the Fugitive Slave Law provides an entirely different proceeding. It authorizes the Court here to try the questions of slavery and escape, as well as identity, in this state, where the escaping person was found.

"Now which proceeding are we under?" Dana asked. "Doubtless under that provided in the Sixth Section. The claimant introduces Mr. Brent, and by him means to prove the fact of slavery, ownership by Colonel Suttle, and the escape. This evidence was not offered to prove identity, but to prove title and escape.

"We say that the two proceedings cannot be combined. The jurisdiction and duties of the Commissioner are different in the two cases."

Dana went on to say that the claimant, Suttle, was free to proceed under either method. And having elected to proceed under Section Six, he could no longer introduce his record under Section Ten. The two methods could not be so combined.

There was a hum of murmurings in the courtroom, but it hushed as Dana pressed forward.

He said that one of the main points of Suttle's case was

147

the *escape*. But had there been any escape? In order for there to be an escape, Dana said, two things had to happen: The person came away of his own will and against his master's will. But Seth Thomas, lawyer for Colonel Suttle, had introduced evidence showing that Burns had not escaped of his own will. So a case of escape had not been made out, Dana said.

Richard Dana then spoke quietly to Commissioner Loring. "I regret, sir, that you did not adopt the rule that in the trial of an issue of freedom, the admissions of the alleged slave while in custody, made to the man who claims him, should not be received by the court. That ruling would have been supported by reason and humanity."

Dana sighed. He had been speaking for a long time. He looked at Anthony Burns and was surprised that Burns was smiling in gratitude. Such dark eyes, so full of hurt and . . . kindness!

He turned back to the Commissioner. "You recognized, sir, in the beginning, the presumption of freedom. Hold to it now, sir. . . . If you commit a mistake in favor of the man, an amount of money, not great, is but at risk. If you rule against him, a free man will be a slave forever.

"The eyes of many millions are upon you, sir," Dana said. "You are to do an act which will hold it place in the history of America, in the history of the progress *of the human race*. May your judgment be for liberty and not for slavery, for hope and not despair."

The face of the Commissioner looked haggard. His

breathing seemed labored. He would not meet Richard Dana's eyes as Dana sat down.

Immediately, Seth Thomas rose to give his closing argument. He would not attempt Dana's eloquence even if he could, but he would do a proper job—this he was sure of.

"The claimant in this case, Charles F. Suttle, says he is of Alexandria, in the State of Virginia; that, under the laws of that state, he held to service and labor one Anthony Burns, a colored man; that, on or about the twenty-fourth day of March last, while so held to service by him, the said Anthony escaped from the said State of Virginia and that he is now here in court. He prays that the Commissioner hear and consider his proofs in support of this claim, that you will certify to him, under your hand and seal, that he has a right to transport Anthony Burns back to Virginia. This is his whole case; this is all that he asks you to do. Under your certificate, he may take Anthony Burns back to the place from whence he fled."

Seth Thomas said for the claimant to be entitled to the certificate, he must prove just two things: that Burns owed service and labor to him and that Burns escaped. He said the transcript of the Virginia record proved both. "One question remains," he said. "Is the person at the bar Anthony Burns—is he the Anthony Burns named in the record? If he is, there is an end of the case. The claim is made out and the certificate must follow.

"In addition to the record and proof of identity, I have deemed it proper to put in the testimony of Mr. Brent, and the admissions of Burns. As to the question of identity, there is the description in the record. And although this has been objected to by the opposing counsel as being loose, I contend that it is sufficiently exact to warrant its exclusive application to the prisoner.

"And to show that Anthony Burns was here on the first of March," said Thomas, "they have put into the case the testimony of one Jones, a colored man, and rely on that. But we believe that his story is manufactured for the case.

"The only one of the witnesses not of their case was Gould, and we called upon him to testify and he directly contradicts Jones. Jones undoubtedly did work at the Mattapan Works and there was, no doubt, another colored man there with him. But it was not Burns. No doubt Whittemore saw Jones there. No doubt he saw the other colored man also. But he never saw Burns there. He is mistaken in the man. That is all. The truth is, Jones went around and asked if some did not remember the man he had with him cleaning the windows; told them the man was Burns, impressed them with this fact. They came into court with this impression and made up their minds that he was. This is the only theory consistent with their honesty.

"Your Honor, this case is proved in three ways—by the record, by the testimony of Brent, and by the admissions of the defendant, either of which ways would alone be sufficient.

"They say these witnesses show that Brent is wrong in testifying that he saw Burns in Virginia on the twentieth. Suppose this to be so; what then? The date is not material. Even a crime of a high nature may be charged to have been done on the twenty-fourth of March, and proved to have been done on the twenty-fourth of February. But our action here is a civil proceeding, not a criminal charge. We seek a remedy distinct from a criminal proceeding. There need be no formal complaint in the case. The complaint is merely the foundation for the warrant. The person escaping may be arrested without a warrant. Brent may possibly be mistaken in the date, but as to the identity of the person, he cannot be. He is as confident now as ever, and does not wish to change his testimony.

"It remains then," Mr. Thomas said, "that I recapitulate the points already stated and leave this arduous and, in some respects, unpleasant case in your hands. I am not conscious of having said or done anything in the course of the examination that need have provoked personal hostility. If I have, it was not so intended. My connection with the case has been strictly professional. The extraordinary bitterness of opposing counsel has not changed my purpose or my direct course.

"The record is conclusive of two facts, that the person owed service and escaped. That record, with the testimony of Brent and the admissions, prove the identity. I take leave of the case, confident in the proofs presented, confident in the majesty of the law, and confident that the determination here will be just."

The court was then adjourned until Friday morning, June second.

19

JUNE 1, 1854

By Thursday, most people hoped that Commissioner Loring would decide in Anthony Burns's favor. Charles Suttle and William Brent, barricaded in the attic of the Revere House, had noticed a change in their own guards. Everyone, it seemed, had sympathy for the slave and not his owner.

"Believe me," Suttle told Brent, "I will be mo' than happy to leave this No'th-of-nothin' place!"

The Reverend Theodore Parker, minister of Tremont Temple, had his doubts that Burns would go free. Driven by his concern, he sat down to compose a leaflet regarding the defense's proof that Burns was in Boston at the time the slave owner claimed he was in Virginia.

"Americans! Freemen!" he wrote.

It has now been established out of the mouths of many witnesses that the poor prisoner now in the Slave Pen, Court Square, is not the slave of the kidnapper, Suttle. Commissioner Loring will doubtless so decide. But will the victim be set free? Believe it not until you see it. The Fugitive Slave Law was framed with a devilish cunning. It allows that if one commissioner refuses to deliver up a man, he may be taken before a second and a third, until someone is found base enough to do the deed.

The leaflet was printed on Thursday and delivered throughout the city and beyond.

Richard Dana had his doubts as well. Although his plea of argument had held the Commissioner's attention, Loring had made no notes as Dana spoke.

Not one note, Dana thought. Not on any of my points about the Virginia record or the escape. He wrote down not a word!

This fact upset him, worrying him throughout the day and well into the night.

In his cell, Anthony Burns leaned his head against the wall and closed his eyes. He was glad that the business in the court was finished. It had been long and tiring. The way Mr. Dana could talk on and on without reading from anything! he thought. Oh, to be able to speak like that. No, better that I preach like that someday. How I wish that was possible! But it seems not to be. No, it does not seem I will go free.

Anthony had noticed that the guard surrounding him had been doubled. Do they think someone will steal me? he wondered. Is there to be another storm against this Court House? When they decide that I shall have to go back, will the people fight against my rendition?

Asa Butman had grown fond of Anthony—Tony, as the

fine Virginia Colonel called him. Oh, yes, Asa decided, I'd take the Colonel over the radicals any day! Colonel and Mr. Brent and their lawyers would surely show Dana and his crew a thing or two. They'd find out that there were still citizens who wouldn't stand for letting black slaves walk about just as they pleased.

The slave Thomas Sims had been made to go back. Oh, there'd been a great row in 1851! Then Asa and his boys had held Sims in the same room where they were now holding Burns. Sims was a lad of seventeen. And he had begged, "Give me a knife, and when the Commissioner declares me a slave, I will stab myself in the heart before his eyes."

Instead, Sims had stabbed Asa. The wound had bled all over, but it hadn't been terrible. Asa'd lived to tell all about it. But the Commissioner had sent Sims back, and rightly, too, Asa believed. He could still hear the hollering of the ab-o-litionists as three hundred policemen surrounding Sims walked him to the ship that would carry him back to bondage—"Sims!" one radical had cried, "preach liberty to the slaves!"

Liberty, indeed! Asa would like to pound every one of them kind to the ground. Let them cry all they want over this slave, too, he thought, looking at Anthony Burns.

Still, Burns was a bit of all right. "He ain't a bad one now, he's not turned sour," Asa had said to the other guards. "An animal can be sniveling, a menace, or brave like a man. I'd say Tony's acting like a man most the time he's been with us. I'd say he's more like one of us than some of the blacks we got up here living free as you please. He can't get away, though, y'know. He can't escape the fate he's born to."

Butman proposed they do something special for Tony. "Here now, let's all give a few dollars, and he can be well turned out."

Asa and his men collected forty dollars. They bought Anthony a new black suit. They presented it to him before he lay down to sleep Thursday night.

Anthony could not believe it. "Try it on, now, Tony," Butman said. "It looks a good fit—try it." Anthony tried it. It fit him well.

"Never in my life!" he murmured, letting his hand slide gingerly down the fine fabric. The suit made him feel almost as good as anyone.

The guards stood around him, smiling. Someone produced a banjo.

"Would you play a little something, Tony?" asked Deputy Riley. It did not occur to him or any of the others that Anthony might not know how to play an instrument.

"Right you are—sing us a tune, Tony," said Butman. "You know, one of them spirituals, just like you do on the plantation."

They think we all know how to sing and play, thought Anthony. There was an awkward silence as he hung his head. The guards waited, shifting their feet.

He hummed a tuneless sound for a few seconds. Then he shook his head.

"Aw, now, m'boy, you're tired out. You've forgotten a lot from down there in all this excitement," Asa said. There were murmurs of agreement from his men. "Well, never you mind it. We're going to see that your last time here is all pleasure."

"Yass, yass!" the men hollered. A few even felt so kindly toward Anthony that they slapped him on the back.

I am to be a slave again, thought Anthony. They know before everyone. He heaved a great sigh. It was as if his mind shut down. No thought, no past, no present moved him to ponder. For with no future, he could not dream. He never uttered another word that night. None of the guards, drinking and reveling, seemed to notice.

Anthony slept fitfully Thursday night. Dark dreams awakened him with a start. For a few seconds he didn't know who he was or what he must do.

Outside, the streets of Boston appeared to be blanketed with winter snow. But this was June, not January. Covering the ground were leaflets from the abolitionist press. They lay abandoned, ragged as fallen flowers after a storm.

Toward the dawn, detachments of soldiers commenced to stir in their armories.

As early as six o'clock a few citizens gathered in Court Square with every intention of staying until Commissioner Loring made his decision. With every hour thereafter the crowd increased. At sunrise a detachment of the Fourth Regiment of U.S. Artillery marched up State Street, transporting with it a field piece, a cannon drawn by two matched horses. Glistening in the morning light, it was placed in the Court Square pointing toward Court Street. Next, the Artillery men were relieved by a detachment of U.S. Marines who stood guard over the cannon.

Before eight o'clock there were three hundred people

156

in the Square. By eight thirty the northern side of Court Street was thronged with people of every complexion, all awaiting the Commissioner's announcement of the decision. Several companies of soldiers, including the Lancers and the Light Dragoons, marched to the parade ground on Boston Common, where they formed into columns. All the troops were under the command of Major General Edmands.

At nine o'clock the bell on the Court House tolled for the opening of the Commissioner's Court. The crowd in Court Square, now a multitude, increased by the minute.

In the courtroom Marshal Freeman's guards were edgy. They could hear the crowd outside, and they held pistols and clubs as, one by one, the lawyers, reporters, privileged spectators, and friends of Anthony Burns took their seats.

Commissioner Loring was seated at the judge's bench. He did not look at anyone in the courtroom. His face was gray and pasty. If he felt all eyes upon him—the stony glare of Reverend Theodore Parker, the patient hopeful look of Reverend Grimes, the impudent stare of Ben Hallett, and the apparent faith in law and order in the expression of Richard Dana—he gave no inkling. Nor did Edward Loring take notice of the prisoner, Anthony Burns. Anthony wore his wonderful dark suit with somber dignity as he sat silently in the prisoner's box.

As he looked around the courtroom, Richard Dana became aware of something incredible. Charles Suttle, William Brent, Suttle's lawyers, and his Southern friends were not in the courtroom.

In the intense quiet, Commissioner Loring began reading his decision. It was long, but he read it firmly and clearly:

"The facts to be proved by the claimant, Charles Suttle, are three," he said. "First, that Anthony Burns owed him service in Virginia. Second, that Anthony Burns escaped from that service. These two facts the claimant has proved, having made satisfactory proof to the Virginia court; whereupon that court caused a record to be made of the matters so proved. But these matters must be tried in the state from which the man escaped. I therefore have no jurisdiction over the facts of the Virginia court record.

"The third fact to be proved is the identity of the prisoner before me with the Anthony Burns mentioned in the record.

"This identity is the only question I have a right to consider. To this I am to apply the evidence. Between the testimony of the claimant, Suttle, and the respondent, Burns, there is a conflict, complete and insolvable: The testimony of the claimant has Anthony Burns of the record in Virginia on the twentieth of March last; the evidence of the respondent has him in Massachusetts on or about the first of March last.

"The question now is, whether there is other evidence in this case which will determine this conflict. In every case of disputed identity there is one person, always, whose knowledge is perfect and positive, and whose evidence is not within the reach of error; and that is the person whose identity is questioned, and such evidence this case affords. The evidence is of the conversation which took place between Burns and the claimant on the night of the arrest.

"When the claimant entered the room where Burns was, Burns saluted him—'How do you do, Master *Charles*?'

"Colonel Suttle said, 'How came you here?' Burns said an accident had happened to him; that he was working on board a vessel, got tired and went to sleep, and was carried off in the vessel. 'Anthony, did I ever whip you?' asked Colonel Suttle—'No, sir.'—'Have you ever asked me for money when I did not give it to you?'—'No, sir.'

"Something was said about going back. Burns was asked if he was willing to go back, and he said, yes he was.

"To me," the Commissioner said, "this evidence, when applied to the question of identity, confirms and establishes the testimony of Mr. Brent in its conflict with that offered on the part of the respondent; and then, on the whole testimony, my mind is satisfied beyond a reasonable doubt of the identity of the respondent with the Anthony Burns named in the record.

"On the law and facts of the case," Loring said, "I consider the claimant entitled to the certificate from me which he claims."

Richard Dana paled. Loring had accepted Burns's alleged admissions to Suttle as evidence, though to do so was *wrong* and unconstitutional. A man was protected from being a witness against himself. He was protected from giving testimony against himself by the Fugitive Slave Act.

Judge Loring gathered his notes and quickly left.

There was a shocked stillness in the courtroom. The spectators were stunned; for a moment nobody moved.

Then the court was ordered cleared, except for Marshal Freeman's guard and the prisoner. Reporters rushed away.

Anthony shrank back into himself. He became once again that picture of despair that Richard Dana had first seen. After he was taken back to his cell, Dana visited Anthony with Reverend Grimes. They stayed with him for an hour, trying to lift his spirits.

"It will be all right, Mr. Burns," Reverend Grimes told him. "The slave owner and the government only want to take you back to Virginia to prove their point. Then we will get you back."

Anthony smiled suddenly. "You would do that for me?" he whispered.

"Of course, and it shall be done," Richard Dana said.

"I was afraid you all would forget about me," Anthony said.

"No," said Dana, "never for a moment. Let me say I am so sorry that it has turned out as it has."

"You did all you could," Anthony said. "And I am grateful to you both. God bless you!" He lifted his mangled hand. "I was afraid they'd sell me to the deep South. With this hand—they'd ill-treat me."

The Marshal's guard stayed close by the whole time Anthony's visitors were there. Asa Butman sidled importantly over to Dana. "Marshal Freeman says yer talks with the prisoner must be in hearing of a guard." He was quite pleased with himself for not having said "Sir" to this learned gentleman.

"Is the order that I must be overheard by this man, and this man, and this man?" Dana asked, pointing to three of the guards.

"These are the orders," Butman said.

"I shall hold no conversation in such company," Dana said. "I shall not consent to hold any conversation with the prisoner on such terms."

Dana shook with anger. He managed to control himself and spoke one last time to Anthony. "Good-bye, Mr. Burns," he said as calmly as he could. "You can be assured, your condition will change for the better, and quite soon."

For the moment, however, Dana felt shaken by all that had happened, and utterly helpless.

"Mr. Burns, here is my address," said Reverend Grimes. "I have also given you the address of Deacon Pitts. Perhaps you will be allowed to write us."

"Yes, I surely will if I am able," Anthony said. He looked earnestly at both Dana and Reverend Grimes. "You did all you could," he said. "I'm well satisfied at that. I thank you with my heart and soul. Thank you!"

They left and walked back and forth for an hour in front of the Court House.

The square was filled with troops. The crowd, thousands strong, had been cleared behind police lines. At Court Street it was a huge, angry mass. If there were those who sided with the Southerners, they were outnumbered by those against slavery and slave capture. When the troops moved at all, the crowd heaved itself forward, hissing and screaming. When it saw Richard Dana and Reverend Grimes leave Court Square, it gave twelve cheers.

The business shops of Court and State Streets were closed. Many were draped in the black cloth of mourning. A coffin had been hung high above State Street with *The*

Funeral of Liberty written on its side. Flags were flown with the union (the section of white stars on a field of blue) pointed down in the universal symbol of a vessel—in this case the Ship of State—in distress. The cannon had been moved from the Square to the very door of the Court House. Now the word spread through the crowd that Anthony would be led away on foot. He would pass down State Street to Long Wharf, where the steamer *John Taylor* waited to take him out to another vessel, the cutter *Morris*. The *Morris*, some distance offshore in the deep channel, would carry Anthony back to Virginia.

20

JUNE 2, 1854

At noon on June 2, 1854, not a cloud marred the blue sky. The sun was bright and warm. Eighteen hundred men of the volunteer militia stood in the sunshine, carrying loaded guns. They were stationed in the streets and lanes all the way from the Court House to Long Wharf. More troops took up positions on either side of State Street, so that in all there were more than two thousand men armed against Anthony Burns. Fifty thousand citizens lined the streets also, hissing and booing every time there was a troop movement.

Inside the Court House the guards tried to cheer Anthony. Deputy Riley gave him four dollars for his journey. "We intend to buy you ourselves, Tony," he said proudly. "We've already collected four hundred dollars, more than you've ever seen, I'll wager. And we mean for every penny to go toward your purchase."

Anthony said not a word.

"All right, boys, it's time," Asa Butman said.

At two o'clock a detachment of United States Artillery gathered in Court Square. Next came a platoon of United

States Marines. Those were followed by the armed posse of Marshal Freeman, and two more platoons of Marines. The cannon that had guarded the entrance to the Court House came up last, with another platoon of Marines in the rear.

When these were ready, Anthony was led from his room flanked by two officers, whose arms were interlocked behind him. He was taken through a corridor lined with soldiers straight to the center of Marshal Freeman's armed posse of 124 men.

Anthony was dressed in his new dark suit. Fine suit for a funeral, he thought, and bowed his head. The long procession started out. The vast throng watching fell silent at the sight of Anthony Burns surrounded. Then it moaned and hissed as he passed them by.

Anthony could barely see the multitude, but he could hear it. It amazed him. He could see clutches of people at every window of the buildings lining the route.

Sure are lots of folks to see a colored man walk down the street, he thought. At the intersection of Washington Street he passed under the coffin labeled *The Funeral of Liberty*. Yea, Lord! he thought.

He and his procession passed the Old State House site, where in 1646 the founding fathers of the Commonwealth of Massachusetts had condemned human slavery.

He walked over the ground where black Crispus Attucks had fallen, the first person to die in the American Revolution.

Up and down the lines, the thousands began to chant "Shame! Shame!" in rhythm with the soldiers' marching.

***

It was a vast, echoing cry that seemed to come from everywhere, the sky and the ground at once.

"Shame! Shame!"

A captain became so angry that he wheeled his horse into the crowd and cut a man with his saber. Another bystander had his head laid open. Soldiers broke the line, assaulting men and women and beating them to the ground.

At Commercial Street the crowd surged forward. Suddenly Lancers attacked, riding their horses straight into the crowd and hacking left and right with their blades. Screams and cries echoed up and down the street as people were trampled under horses' hooves.

All at once, some soldiers began singing "Carry Me Back to Old Virginny." They kept on singing all the way to the Wharf. There Anthony, Asa Butman, Deputy Riley, and many others who had marched from Court Square were put aboard the *John Taylor*.

It reminded many of '51 and Thomas Sims, and hundreds were brought to tears.

Church bells in the vicinity began a sad tolling, and soon bells chimed all over Boston. The mournful toll rang out from town to town, from Plymouth to Salem, to Haverhill and on. Throughout the coast of New England, it was as if the hills chimed:

Anthony Burns is taken back to slavery. We toll for him and thee. And for shame, and shame again.

ANTHONY WAS led into a cabin of the *Morris*, and there was Colonel Suttle waiting for him. Suttle and Brent had left their hotel at dawn on the day of the trial and been taken to the Navy Yard at Charlestown. There they had been transported in secret to the cutter. It would seem they had known Commissioner Loring's decision before Loring had told it to the court.

The Colonel nodded curtly to Anthony and at once got down to business.

"I want the name of the ship's captain who brought you to Boston," he said. "I'll give you your freedom if you tell me his name."

"But I don't know," Anthony said. "I never seen the captain at all on the ship."

"Well, if I knew the scoundrel, he wouldn't ever want to carry off another Negro," said Suttle. "I would put him in the penitentiary for life."

Suttle and Brent soon left the ship.

Anthony remained under guard for eight days until his arrival in Norfolk.

Once on land in Norfolk, Anthony was put in jail for two days. He had no bed or chair in his cell and was given only one meal in that time. From this beginning, Anthony knew he would be made an example of. He steadied and strengthened himself with prayer as best he could.

The ship voyage continued, and then he was again thrown in jail on reaching Richmond, Virginia. There he stayed for ten days, until William Brent came to see him. With Brent was Robert Lumpkin, a well-known trader of slaves. He kept a trader's jail, where he boarded slaves until they were sold. He also kept slaves for owners who wished to have them punished. Brent handed Anthony over to Robert Lumpkin for a four-month stay. Thus began Anthony's sentence for committing the crime of running away.

Lumpkin's jail was a three-story brick building on an acre of land at the edge of Richmond. The property was surrounded by a high fence with iron spikes at the top. The jail was quite solid and secure. There was no chance of escape.

Anthony was handcuffed with his hands behind him and taken to the very top of the jail. There he was put into a tiny room that could be reached only through a trapdoor. The room had a bench, with a thin blanket lying on it, against the wall. Anthony's feet and hands were chained. And that was the way he lived for most of the next four months.

The iron shackles were tight and painful. The room was stiflingly hot. The skin covering Anthony's feet and ankles slowly began to feel tight. He watched, amazed, as his feet swelled to such a huge size that they were hardly recognizable as feet. They itched so, he feared his skin would burst. And his wrists were bloody now from the handcuffs biting into his flesh. The pain was unbearable.

The cell was soon a revolting place to be, foul smelling from his excrement. Rats and insects scurried through the filth.

"Oh, God. God, save me," moaned Anthony. "Let me die."

He was given one meal a day—a chunk of cornbread, a little bacon or half-rotted meat. He was forced to gobble the mess like an animal off the floor. Once a week a guard brought him a bucket of water.

Anthony became so seriously ill that his handcuffs and

foot irons were removed for a short time. To keep him alive, he was fed rich broth. Every day when he was well enough, he was brought down to the grounds of the jail and put on display. Thirty or so people came each time to look at him, kneeling in his cage.

He was the zoo animal, the "Boston Lion." Folks cursed him and laughed at him. After an hour or two of this daily humiliation, he was returned to his cell and the irons were placed on his hands and feet again.

One day, after Anthony had lost all track of time, the torture abruptly ended. Now, suddenly, he had enough to eat—good meat and bread. The swelling in his feet went down, but it remained somewhat difficult for him to walk. He never felt entirely well. But he tried as best he could to stand tall and appear healthy. It was not long before he was taken to the Richmond auction block for sale.

Anthony saw Colonel Suttle there, watching. Suttle started yelling in a loud voice, "My nigguh won't be sold to no damn Yankee! No, suh!"

Other Southern gentlemen made angry speeches against Anthony, the disgusting slave who had run away from his kind owner. And the bidding for him went slowly. There were not many slavers who wanted a runaway slave.

Finally, Anthony was sold for $905 to David McDaniel of Rocky Mount, North Carolina. Fearing that his newly purchased slave might be lynched, McDaniel took Anthony and left Richmond under cover of darkness.

McDaniel had a large plantation. He was a cotton planter, a horse dealer, and a slave trader combined. He gave Anthony the job of coachman and stable keeper for the carriage horses and for McDaniel's own riding filly.

Anthony did not stay with the hundreds of slaves in the slave quarters, but slept in the plantation office in a room he shared with the white overseer. He was permitted to take what food he needed from a store owned by McDaniel, and he ate his meals in McDaniel's house.

So it was that his fortunes had changed again. Least I'm not whipped, I'm not starved half to death, Anthony thought. He did his job and kept to himself for many months. No one will ever find me, he thought. His Northern friends had no idea what had become of him; all their efforts to trace his whereabouts had been futile.

One day Anthony drove Mrs. McDaniel in her carriage to the home of a neighbor. He was pointed out as the runaway slave who had excited the whole country. A young woman wrote her sister in Massachusetts about the "Boston Lion." The sister in turn told the story to her circle of friends, where a Reverend G. S. Stockwell overheard the tale. He at once addressed a letter to the slave owner, McDaniel, asking to buy Anthony. Immediately McDaniel wrote back stating that Anthony Burns could be purchased for thirteen hundred dollars. Reverend Stockwell informed Reverend Grimes of Anthony's whereabouts. Quickly, the two men went about raising the money for Anthony's release.

"I'm going to tell you a secret," McDaniel said to Anthony one day. "You must tell no one, not even my wife." He told Anthony to be ready on Monday, for they were going to Baltimore.

"Suh, you are going to sell me South?" Anthony cried. "Didn't I do my job good? I'll make it right, suh, I surely will, just give me another chance."

169

"No, now listen to me," McDaniel said. "There's a Reverend Stockwell with a Reverend Grimes . . ."

"Reverend Grimes!" Anthony interrupted. His heart leaped.

"Yes. We're to meet them on the twenty-seventh of February in Baltimore. They have your freedom!"

"Oh, Lord of mercy!" whispered Anthony. It was another year then, 1855. And another attempt at free-dom.

Again McDaniel swore him to secrecy, for he risked jail and perhaps his life in sending Anthony North; any aid in the rescue of a slave was a crime under the Fugitive Slave Act. Monday morning came and the two men boarded a train. Anthony slumped his shoulders so he wouldn't appear so tall. He hid his maimed hand as best he could. Still, people noticed him. They had not gone ten miles before it was known that the fugitive slave the "Boston Lion" was on the train.

"I demand this nigguh be stopped and put off," a gentleman exclaimed to the conductor. "He's got the runaway disease; I don't want my slaves to catch it."

Coolly, McDaniel pulled out his pistol. "I will put a bullet in the first person who lays a hand on my property," he said.

Nobody moved. The protesting Southern gentleman backed away. The conductor went on about his business. And in this way, McDaniel kept the passengers in check all the way to Norfolk.

On arrival there they boarded a steamer that was leaving for Baltimore later in the day. But meanwhile, the train passengers had spread the word that Anthony was in Baltimore and heading North. In no time the ship was swarming with angry citizens. McDaniel sent Anthony below deck, and for three hours he staved off the mob with his pistol pointed at them.

"I offer you fifteen hundred dollars for him," a man said. "Please, don't sell your slave No'th. They will free him there and make a hero out of him. He needs to be disciplined for his crime."

"If my purchasers fail to keep their appointment in Baltimore, why then I will sell him to you," McDaniel said.

Finally, the steamer left Norfolk. Anthony and David McDaniel went on without further trouble.

In Baltimore they stayed at Barnum's Hotel, which was owned by the great showman P. T. Barnum. There Anthony was greeted by Reverend Grimes. He and the reverend embraced, for the moment speechless with happiness. The money was paid to McDaniel out of Anthony's sight, and the slaver went on his way.

"I knew one day you'd find me," Anthony said to Reverend Grimes.

"I knew I would find you too, for I could not rest until I did," said the good reverend.

The rumor that Anthony was in the city had spread all over town. "We have to get you out of here right away," Reverend Stockwell said. He and Mr. Grimes and Anthony headed at once for the railway station. There they found that a bond of one thousand dollars had to be posted for a black leaving the state. The bond was necessary so that the company could not be sued for "carrying Negroes."

P. T. Barnum signed the bond. And with this last obstacle out of the way, Anthony left the land of slavery forever. When he arrived North, he was famous. People everywhere wanted to hear his story and to shake his hand. He was asked to speak in lecture halls in New York, in Boston, and throughout the state of Massachusetts. Wherever he appeared, the public came out to hear him and to give him their sympathy.

Anthony would delicately hold his wrists and say, "I was kept for months with bracelets on these. Not such as you wear, ladies, of gold and silver, but iron and steel that wore into the bone." The newspapers printed all he said with generally favorable comments—so much so that Mr. Barnum offered Anthony five hundred dollars if he would stand in the Museum of New York and tell his story to visitors for a period of five weeks.

Anthony was horrified. "He wants to show me like a monkey!" he said, and refused the offer. Not wanting to spend his life as a traveling lecturer, he wished to attend college and become a proper minister. When a Boston woman generously offered him a scholarship to Oberlin College in Ohio, Tony gratefully accepted. Meantime, a writer called Charles Emery Stevens decided to write Anthony's biography, which he did, with Anthony's aid. The book, entitled *Anthony Burns, A History*, was published in 1856, and a large portion of the sales went to further Anthony's education.

During his two years at Oberlin Anthony was often ill, and he so wrote the Reverend Grimes, who still kept in touch with him. For a short time later, he was in charge of a "colored" Baptist church in Indianapolis, Indiana. But he was forced to leave by the threat of enforcement of the state's Black Laws, which restricted the lives of blacks and even their settlement in the state.

I will go to Canada! Anthony decided. Knowing that he would be safe there, for that was the final run for many fugitives, he left the "free-dom" of the American North. He moved at last to the small settlement of St. Catharines, Canada, on the south shore of Lake Ontario, and became the pastor of Zion Baptist Church.

Tall and well mannered, Anthony became quite a good speaker. He was much loved by his parishioners. He never loved another, as he said he wouldn't. He never married, but he was happy, preaching the gospel and seeing to the needs of his flock. Yet it was not long before his health broke completely. The great hardship he had suffered over many years, ending with the final assault in the Lumpkin jail, took its final toll. He fell ill, was confined to bed for a month, and then died on July 27, 1862.

"He was a fine-looking man," said another minister, Reverend R. A. Ball. "He was tall and broad-shouldered, but with a slight stoop. His color was light brown. He was a fine speaker and was considered to be well educated, and very popular with both white people and the people of his own race."

A St. Catharines newspaper gave this report:

The best medical aid was procured, but that most uncompromising and wasting disease, consumption, had taken a fast hold of Anthony Burns and all that human skill could do failed to wrest the sufferer from its grasp.

Reverend Burns had been here only a short time. When he came, he saw that there was much for him to do and he set himself to do it with all his heart, and he was prospering in his work, he was getting the affairs of the church into good shape. His memory will be cherished long by not a few in this town. His gentle, unassuming and yet manly bearing secured him many friends. His removal is felt to be a great loss and his place will not soon be filled.

On his grave is this stone with the inscription:

In Memoriam
REV. ANTHONY BURNS
The fugitive slave of the Boston riots, 1854.
Pastor of Zion Baptist Church
Died in the Triumph of Faith in St. Catharines,
July 27th A.D. 1862

Anthony died only twenty-eight years old. And yet he had lived a life that would have overwhelmed most men. He hated human slavery. But through it all, he never lost his faith in people and his belief in God. He cherished free-dom to the last.

EPILOGUE

IN THE AUTUMN OF 1854 Reverend Theodore Parker, Wendell Phillips, Thomas Wentworth Higginson, Martin Stowell, and others were indicted by a grand jury for "knowingly and willfully obstructing, resisting and opposing" a United States Marshal in "the discharge of his lawful duties."

On April 3, 1855, the Court pronounced all the indictments lacking. The U.S. District Attorney, Benjamin Hallett, was then unwilling to prosecute further, and the suit against the accused individuals was dropped.

The extradition of Anthony Burns was the immediate cause for legislation called the Personal Liberty Law, passed in Massachusetts on May 21, 1855. The Law guaranteed that no individual could be arrested and thrown into jail without first going before a judge or a court to determine whether his arrest had been justified. This right of *habeas corpus* is a safeguard against illegal detention or imprisonment.

The slave struggle continued in the North and South. But Anthony Burns was the last fugitive ever seized on Massachusetts soil.

Afterword

MORE THAN ten years ago I began putting together source material on an ordinary slave. He escaped from bondage only to be recaptured, and thus galvanized and unified the antislavery movement. This fugitive slave became famous in the process and now is dutifully mentioned in most of our history books.

Once I involved myself in researching the man's life, I felt that he somehow deserved more than a paragraph or a mere mention in the historical references on Slavery, Abolitionist Causes, and Famous Fugitives.

It was not until 1985, though, that I had the opportunity to reconstruct the fugitive's life and times as an in-depth biography. *Anthony Burns: The Defeat and Triumph of a Fugitive Slave* is the result.

Anthony Burns is a narrative history of events surrounding Anthony's life as well as a biography. In the research material, however, there existed no day-to-day calendar of events to outline Burns's activities and movement as an ordinary slave child and youth. His life only became well documented from approximately his twentieth year, when he was hired out to Richmond, Virginia, and carefully began to plan his escape.

Therefore it became necessary to invent and "backfill" from this later material.

Various documents place Anthony Burns at the Hiring Ground over several years in his youth and state that he was in charge of other slaves. Anthony was actually hired out to the individual slave owners as described here. It is also true that his hand was horribly mangled while he was employed by a Mr. Foote. As a result of the torture and pain of his wound, he had several religious experiences and became quite devout.

However, the slave owner who hired Whittom and Simon is an invention, as are the slave owners Archibald Davenport and Ebenezer Caldwell and the four slaves in Anthony's charge—Whittom, Efrum, Luther, and Simon.

There are five shadowy but actual people who were in some way important in Anthony's development but who are only mentioned occasionally in the documentation of his life. These people are referred to in the documentary material as Anthony's "mother," who tried to keep him safe with her and wanted him to grow up to be a preacher; "a sailor," who helped Anthony escape to the North; Anthony's "older sister," whose baby was in Anthony's care; "a seer and fortuneteller," who predicted Anthony would go free; and Anthony's "father," who died when he was quite young. In the absence of documents citing the real names of these individuals, I have given them names: Mamaw for Anthony's "mother," Cal Cross for "a sailor," Sister Janety for Anthony's "older sister," Maude Maw for "a seer and fortuneteller," and Big Walker for Anthony's "father." I have also given them active roles in his life, drawing from whatever supporting factual material was available.

The remaining individuals in the list of characters are real people who were known in Burns's time. Some were famous then and are still historically significant: P. T. Barnum, Richard Dana, Cyrus Gould, Samuel G. Howe, Thomas Higginson, Theodore Parker, President Franklin Pierce, Wendell Phillips, Shadrach, and Thomas Sims. Some are generally unknown now but we should take note of their courage: Charles Mayo Ellis, Leonard Grimes, William Jones, Coffin Pitts, and Martin Stowell. Others were relatively unknown at the time but will be infamous always: Asa Butman, Mr. and Mrs. Foote, Charles Suttle, John and Mistress Suttle, Ben Hallett, and Robert Lumpkin. Still others, such as Edward Loring, David McDaniel, George Drew, and John Favor, were in many ways captured by events. Whatever marks of character they possessed—strengths or weaknesses—were revealed under the pressure of circumstance.

You might ask, What does the life of a slave born a hundred and fifty years ago have to do with us? Here was a poor fugitive who lived but nine years of his total life of twenty-eight years in freedom. Yet he did become free, and he died a free man, so why not let it go at that? What does a single slave out of millions like him, long gone and best forgotten, have to do with us—you, me—in this last decade before the year 2000?

Today readers of *Anthony Burns* enjoy an inalienable right to freedom and the pursuit of happiness given to them by the Constitution and its amendments. Such an assumption of liberty was unknown to those captured by a tragically cruel system of human servitude. Ultimately Anthony Burns did know freedom, but at a regrettable cost to himself, mentally and physically.

As the author of this life of Anthony Burns, I have experienced an enormous sense of relief and satisfaction at having at last set free through the word one man's struggle for liberty. All these years Anthony Burns has lived in my thoughts: this man, born a slave, whose painstaking and burning desire to "get gone" from crippling bondage was all but forgotten by history. By writing about him I found that he not only came to life for me but that he lives again for all of us. In gaining a sense of who he was we learn about ourselves. As long as we know he is free, we too are liberated.

One last word should be given with regard to those abolitionist advocates, witnesses, and lawyers in the cause of freedom for slaves, and particularly in the cause of Anthony Burns. If I emphasize Anthony Burns and the work of such humble souls as Reverend Grimes and Coffin Pitts more than the abolitionists and their efforts, it is because most of the famed among the abolitionists have long since written about their lives: Thomas Higginson, Wendell Phillips, Richard Dana, Theodore Parker, and others have all produced monographs or autobiographies that, somewhat incidentally, tell us what they did on behalf of Anthony Burns. In their own works these men are justifiably the center of events. In their accounts of the great abolitionist cause, the swirling intrigues surrounding Burns, and the battle between freedom and slavery, Burns seems to recede into the shadows.

For once I wanted readers to have a book in which the oppressed slave, a common man, was at the center of his own struggle.

VIRGINIA HAMILTON
New York City
December 1987

Selections from the

Fugitive Slave Act
of 1850

The Act amended the original law of 1793, entitled *"An Act respecting Fugitives from Justice, and Persons escaping from the Service of their Masters,"* approved February 12, 1793.

The Fugitive Slave Act was part of the formula in the Compromise of 1850 for settling differences between North and South. The Compromise included the admission of California as free state, the Texas and New Mexico Act, the Utah Act, the Fugitive Slave Act, and an Act Abolishing the Slave Trade in the District of Columbia.

Sections of the Fugitive Slave Act pertinent to *Anthony Burns* follow.

SEC. 5.   That it shall be the duty of all marshals and deputy marshals to obey and execute all warrants and precepts issued under the provisions of this act, when to them directed; and should any marshal or deputy marshal refuse to receive such warrant, or other process, when tendered, or to use all proper means diligently to execute the same, he shall, on conviction thereof, be fined in the sum of one thousand dollars, to the use of such claimant, . . . and after arrest of such fugitive, by such marshal or his deputy, or whilst at any time in his custody under the provisions of this act, should such fugitive escape, whether with or without the assent of such marshal or his deputy, such marshal shall be liable, on his official bond, to be prosecuted for the benefit of such claimant, for the full value of the service or labor of said fugitive in the State, Territory or District whence he or she escaped: and the better to enable the said commissioners, when thus appointed, to execute their duties faithfully and efficiently, in conformity with the requirements of the Constitution of the United States and of this act, they are hereby authorized and empowered, within their counties respectively, to appoint . . . any one or more suitable persons, from time to time, to execute all such warrants and other process as may be issued by them in the lawful performance of their respective duties; with authority to such commissioners, or the persons to be appointed by them, to execute process as aforesaid, to summon and call to their aid the bystanders, or *posse comitatus* of the proper county, when necessary to ensure a faithful observance of the clause of the Constitution referred to, in conformity with the provisions of this act; and all good citizens are hereby commanded to aid and assist in the prompt and efficient execution of this law, whenever their services may be required, as aforesaid, for that purpose; and said warrants shall run, and be executed by said officers, any where in the State within which they are issued.

SEC. 6.   That when a person held to service or labor in a State or Territory of the United States, has heretofore or shall hereafter escape into another State or Territory of the United States, the person or persons to whom such service or labor may be due . . . may pursue and reclaim such fugitive person, either by procuring a warrant from some one of the courts, judges, or commissioners aforesaid, of the proper circuit, district, or county, for the apprehension of such fugitive from service or labor, or by seizing and arresting such fugitive, where the same can be done without process, and by taking, or causing such person to be taken, forthwith before such court, judge, or commissioner, whose duty it shall be to hear and determine the case of such claimant in a summary manner; and upon satisfactory proof being made, by deposition or affidavit, in writing, to be taken and certified by such court, judge, or commissioner, or by other satisfactory testimony, duly taken and certified by some court, . . . and with proof, also by affidavit, of the identity of the person whose service or labor is claimed to be due as aforesaid, that the person so arrested does in fact owe service or labor to the person or persons claiming him or her, in the State or Territory from which such fugitive may have escaped as aforesaid, and that said person escaped, to make out and deliver to such claimant, his agent or attorney, a certificate setting forth the substantial facts as to the service or labor due from such fugitive to the claimant, and of his or her escape from the State or Territory in which he or she was arrested, with authority to such claimant . . . to use such reasonable force and restraint as may be necessary, under the circumstances of the case, to take and remove such fugitive person back to the State or Territory whence he or she may have escaped as aforesaid. In no trial or hearing under this act shall the testimony of such alleged fugitive be admitted in evidence; and the certificates in this . . . section shall be conclusive of the right of the person or persons in whose favor granted, to remove such fugitive to the State or Territory from which he or she escaped, and shall prevent all molestation of such person or persons by any process issued by any court, judge, magistrate, or other person whomsoever.

SEC. 7. That any persons who shall knowingly and willingly obstruct, hinder, or prevent such claimant, his agent or attorney, or any person or persons lawfully assisting him, her, or them, from arresting such a fugitive from service or labor, either with or without process as aforesaid, or shall rescue, or attempt to rescue, such fugitive from service or labor, from the custody of such claimant, . . . or other person or persons lawfully assisting as aforesaid, when so arrested, . . . or shall aid, abet, or assist such person, . . . directly or indirectly, to escape from such claimant, . . . or shall harbor or conceal such fugitive, . . . shall, for either of said offences, be subject to a fine not exceeding one thousand dollars, and imprisonment not exceeding six months . . . ; and shall moreover forfeit and pay, by way of civil damages to the party injured by such illegal conduct, the sum of one thousand dollars, for each fugitive so lost as aforesaid. . . .

SEC. 9. That, upon affidavit made by the claimant of such fugitive, . . . that he has reason to apprehend that such fugitive will be rescued by force from his or their possession before he or she can be taken beyond the limits of the State in which the arrest is made, it shall be the duty of the officer making the arrest to retain such fugitive in his custody, and to remove him or her to the State whence he or she fled, and there to deliver him or her to said claimant, his agent, or attorney. And to this end, the officer aforesaid is hereby authorized and required to employ so many persons as he may deem necessary to overcome such force, and to retain them in his service so long as circumstances may require. . . .

SEC. 10. That when any person held to service or labor in any State or Territory, or in the District of Columbia, shall escape therefrom, the party to whom such service or labor shall be due . . . may apply to any court of record therein . . . and make satisfactory proof to such court . . . of the escape aforesaid, and that the person escaping owed service or labor to such party. Whereupon the court shall cause a record to be made of the matters so proved, and also a general description of the person so escaping, with such convenient certainty as may be; and a transcript of such record . . . being produced in any other State, Territory, or district in which the person so escaping may be found . . . shall be held and taken to be full and conclusive evidence of the fact of escape, and that the service or labor of the person escaping is due to the party in such record mentioned. And upon the production by the said party of other and further evidence if necessary, either oral or by affidavit, in addition to what is contained in the said record of the identity of the person escaping, he or she shall be delivered up to the claimant. And the said court, commissioner, judge, or other person authorized by this act to grant certificates to claimants of fugitives, shall, upon the production of the record and other evidences aforesaid, grant to such claimant a certificate of his right to take any such person identified and proved to be owing service or labor as aforesaid, which certificate shall authorize such claimant to seize or arrest and transport such person to the State or Territory from which he or she escaped. . . .

Summary entry excerpted from *Encyclopedia of American History* (edited by Richard B. Morris, copyright © 1953 by Harper & Row, Inc.; reprinted by permission of the publisher):

[P]laced fugitive slave cases under exclusive Federal jurisdiction; provided for special U.S. commissioners who were authorized, following a summary hearing, to issue warrants for the arrest of fugitives and certificates for returning them to their masters. An affidavit by the claimant was accepted as sufficient proof of ownership. A feature of the law that abolitionists regarded as especially prejudicial was the authorization of a $10 fee for commissioners when such a certificate was granted, and of only $5 when it was refused. The commissioners were authorized to call to their aid bystanders, or to summon a *posse comitatus*, when deemed necessary for enforcing the law. Fugitives claiming to be freemen were denied the right of trial by jury, and their testimony was not to be admitted as evidence at any of the proceedings under the law. Heavy penalties were provided for evasion or obstruction. Marshals and deputies refusing to execute warrants were liable to a $1,000 fine; and in cases where the fugitives escaped through official negligence, the marshal might be sued for the value of the slave. Citizens preventing the arrest of a fugitive, or aiding in his concealment or rescue, were subject to a fine of $1,000, imprisonment up to six months, and civil damages of $1,000 for each fugitive so lost.

Note: A *posse comitatus* was the Marshal's guard, and in the Burns case included Butman, Riley, and others. It was much the same as a posse in the old West, or even like those of today.

Bibliography

Annals of America, The. Vol. 8, *A House Dividing, 1850–1857.* "Horace Mann: Slavery in the Territories," pp. 7–15; "The Compromise of 1850," pp. 52–58; "Richard Baker: The Crime of Mrs. Douglass in Teaching Colored Children to Read," pp. 224–26; "Opposition to the Kansas-Nebraska Bill," pp. 251–54; "Stephen A. Douglas: Defense of the Kansas-Nebraska Bill," pp. 254–60; "Abraham Lincoln: Against the Extension of Slavery," pp. 276–82. Chicago: Encyclopaedia Britannica, Inc., 1968.

BARTLETT, IRVING H. *Wendell and Ann Phillips: The Community of Reform, 1840–1880.* New York: Norton, 1979.

BENNETT, LERONE, JR. *Before the Mayflower: A History of Black America.* Chicago: Johnson Publishing Co., 1982.

BLASSINGAME, JOHN W. *The Slave Community.* New York: Oxford University Press, 1979.

Boston Slave Riot and Trial of Anthony Burns: Transcripts from newspaper reports containing the report of the Faneuil Hall Meeting; The Murder of Bachelder; Theodore Parker's Lesson For the Day; The speeches of Counsel on Both Sides, Corrected by Themselves; A verbatim Report of Judge Loring's

Decision and Detailed Account of the Embarkation. Boston: Fetridge and Co., 1854.

FLETCHER, R. S. *A History of Oberlin College.* 2 vols. Oberlin, Ohio: Oberlin College, 1943.

GRAY, E. H. *Assaults upon Freedom: A Discourse Occasioned by the Rendition of Anthony Burns.* Shelburne Falls, Mass.: D. B. Gunn, 1854.

HIGGINSON, THOMAS WENTWORTH. *Cheerful Yesterdays.* Boston: Houghton Mifflin, 1899.

LANDON, FRED. "Anthony Burns in Canada," in *Papers and Records of the Ontario Historical Society,* vol. 22, pp. 162–66. Ontario: Ontario Historical Society, 1925.

Letters from Anthony Burns. From Jail to Reverend Grimes, May 24, 1854; From Amherst, Mass., to Reverend Grimes, March 27, 1855; to Reverend Grimes, April 10, 1855; to Charles Emery Stevens, July 20, 1855. Oberlin, Ohio: Oberlin College Archives.

MORRIS, RICHARD B., ed. *Encyclopedia of American History.* New York: Harper Brothers, 1953.

NELSON, TRUMAN. *The Sin of the Prophet.* Boston: Little, Brown, 1952.

Oberlin College Archives. Documentary reports and research on Anthony Burns, 1855–62, 1907, 1931, 1967.

PARKER, THEODORE. *A Discourse of Matters Pertaining to Religion,* 4th ed. New York: Putnam, 1876.

PHILLIPS, WENDELL. *Speeches, Lectures and Letters.* Boston: Lee and Shepard, 1884.

PLOSKI, H. A., and BROWN, ROSCOE C., JR. *The Negro Almanac.* New York: Bellwether Publishing Co., 1967.

STEVENS, CHARLES EMERY. *Anthony Burns: A History.* Boston: John P. Jewett and Co., 1856.

Trowbridge, John Townsend. *My Own Story: With Recollections of Noted Persons*. Boston: Houghton Mifflin, 1903.

Ulrich, Bonnell. *Prophet of Liberty: Wendell Phillips*. New York: Bookman Associates, 1958.

Index

VIRGINIA HAMILTON

is one of the most distinguished writers of fiction for children today. *M.C. Higgins the Great* was awarded more honors the year it was published than any other children's book, including the John Newbery Medal, the Boston Globe–Horn Book Award, and the National Book Award. Both *The Planet of Junior Brown* and *Sweet Whispers, Brother Rush* were Newbery Honor Books; the latter won the Boston Globe–Horn Book Award and the Coretta Scott King Award as well. She is also the recipient of the Edgar Allan Poe Award for the best juvenile mystery for *The House of Dies Drear*, and her collection of American black folk tales, *The People Could Fly*, an ALA Notable Children's Book, won her a second Coretta Scott King Award, as well as many other honors.

Virginia Hamilton is married to the poet Arnold Adoff. They make their home in Ohio.